129

134

COLLECTIONS
FOR YOUNG SCHOLARS™
VOLUME 2 BOOK 2

Responsibility

Appearances

Our Country: The Early Years

Our Country: E Pluribus Unum

Art by Lydia Dabcovitch

COLLECTIONS FOR YOUNG SCHOLARS™

VOLUME 2 BOOK 2

PROGRAM AUTHORS
Carl Bereiter
Ann Brown
Marlene Scardamalia
Valerie Anderson
Joe Campione

CONSULTING AUTHORS
Michael Pressley
Iva Carruthers
Bill Pinkney

OPEN COURT PUBLISHING COMPANY
CHICAGO AND PERU, ILLINOIS

CHAIRMAN
M. Blouke Carus

PRESIDENT
André W. Carus

EDUCATION DIRECTOR
Carl Bereiter

CONCEPT
Barbara Conteh

EXECUTIVE EDITOR
Shirley Graudin

MANAGING EDITOR
Sheelagh McGurn

SENIOR PROJECT EDITOR
Nancy Johnson

PROJECT EDITOR
Ana Tiesman

ART DIRECTOR
John Grandits

VICE-PRESIDENT, PRODUCTION
AND MANUFACTURING
Chris Vancalbergh

PERMISSIONS COORDINATOR
Diane Sikora

COVER ARTIST
Lydia Dabcovitch

≥ 4

Printed in the United States of America

ISBN 0-8126-2248-0

10 9 8

ACKNOWLEDGMENTS

Grateful acknowledgment is given to the following publishers and copyright owners for permission granted to reprint selections from their publications. All possible care has been taken to trace ownership and secure permission for each selection included.

Appleton-Century Books: "The Foolish, Timid Rabbit" from *Jataka Tales*, retold by Ellen C. Babbitt, copyright 1912 by The Century Co., copyright 1940 by D. Appleton-Century Co., Inc.

Carolrhoda Books, Inc., Minneapolis, MN: *Squanto and the First Thanksgiving* by Joyce Kessel, illustrated by Lisa Donze, copyright © 1983 by Carolrhoda Books, Inc. *Buttons for General Washington* by Peter and Connie Roop, illustrated by Peter E. Hanson, copyright © 1986 by Carolrhoda Books, Inc.

Dutton Children's Books, a division of Penguin Books USA Inc.: *Watch the Stars Come Out* by Riki Levinson, illustrated by Diane Goode, text copyright © 1985 by Riki Friedberg Levinson, illustrations copyright © 1985 by Diane Goode.

Garrard Publishing Co.: "The First Fourth of July" from *Fourth of July: A Holiday Book* by Charles P. Graves, copyright © 1963 by Charles P. Graves.

Harcourt Brace Jovanovich, Inc.: "Buffalo Dusk" from *Smoke and Steel* by Carl Sandburg, copyright 1920 by Harcourt Brace Jovanovich, Inc., renewed 1948 by Carl Sandburg.

HarperCollins Publishers: *How We Learned the Earth Is Round* by Patricia G. Lauber, illustrated by Megan Lloyd, text copyright © 1990 by Patricia G. Lauber, illustrations copyright © 1990 by Megan Lloyd.

Holiday House, Inc.: "Abraham Lincoln" from *A Picture Book of Abraham Lincoln* by David A. Adler, illustrated by John and Alexandra Wallner, text copyright © 1989 by David A. Adler, illustrations copyright © 1989 by John and Alexandra Wallner. "Martin Luther King, Jr." from *A Picture Book of Martin Luther King, Jr.* by David A. Adler, illustrated by Robert Casilla, text copyright © 1989 by David A. Adler, illustrations copyright © 1989 by Robert Casilla.

Houghton Mifflin Co.: *The Emperor's New Clothes* by Hans Christian Andersen, retold by Virginia Lee Burton, copyright 1949 by Virginia Lee Demetrios, copyright © renewed 1977 by George Demetrios.

Alfred A. Knopf, Inc.: "The Pudding Like a Night on the Sea" from *The Stories Julian Tells* by Ann Cameron, illustrated by Ann Strugnell, text copyright © 1981 by Ann Cameron, illustrations copyright © 1981 by Ann Strugnell. *Follow the Dream* by Peter Sis, copyright © 1991 by Peter Sis.

Little, Brown and Co. and Walker Books Limited: "The Boy Who Cried Wolf," "The Grasshopper and the Ants," and "The Fox and the Crow" from *The Best of Aesop's Fables*, retold by Margaret Clark, illustrated by Charlotte Voake, text copyright © 1990 by Margaret Clark, illustrations copyright © 1990 by Charlotte Voake.

Pantheon Books, a division of Random House, Inc.: *The First Americans* by Jane Werner Watson, illustrated by Troy Howell, copyright © 1982 by Random House, Inc.

Philomel Books: *A Pair of Red Clogs* by Masako Matsuno, illustrated by Kazue Mizumura, text copyright © 1960, 1988 by Masako Matsuno, illustrations copyright © 1960, 1988 by Kazue Mizumura.

Random House, Inc.: *The Pioneers* by Marie and Douglas Gorsline, copyright © 1978 by Douglas Gorsline and Marie Gorsline.

Marian Reiner, for the author: "Waking" from *I Feel the Same Way* by Lilian Moore, copyright © 1967 by Lilian Moore.

Viking Penguin, a division of Penguin Books USA Inc.: *Crow Boy* by Taro Yashima, copyright 1955 by Mitsu and Taro Yashima, copyright © renewed 1983 by Mitsu and Taro Yashima.

Frederick Warne & Co.: *The Tale of Peter Rabbit* by Beatrix Potter, copyright 1902, copyright © 1987 by Frederick Warne & Co. Frederick Warne is the owner of all right, copyrights, and trademarks in the Beatrix Potter character names and illustrations.

Photography
49 Hulton Picture Library/Bettmann

5

RESPONSIBILITY

7 🔥

APPEARANCES

9 ⤳

OUR COUNTRY: THE EARLY YEARS

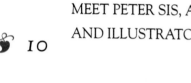 10

OUR COUNTRY: *E PLURIBUS UNUM*

13 🍂

RESPONSIBILITY

15 ❧

CHORES

WASH THE DOG
BRUSH THE DOG
WALK THE DOG
FEED THE DOG
CLEAN THE DOG PEN
PLAY WITH THE DOG

A PAIR OF RED CLOGS

Masako Matsuno
illustrated by Kazue Mizumura

A pair of old cracked wooden clogs!
I found them last night in a storeroom of my house
when I was looking for a box to send a new pair of clogs
to my little granddaughter.

The new pair is painted with red lacquer,
and they shine beautifully.
The old pair is also painted with red lacquer,
and they, too, shone beautifully when they were new.
When the old pair was new,
I was as young as my granddaughter is now.

One evening, when I was as young as my granddaughter is now, I went shopping with my mother. In the small town in the country where we lived, there were many stores along the main street. At the end of the street, there was a small tobacco shop with a red-painted postbox in front. I loved to go into this shop, because wooden clogs were sold there, too. I was going to choose a pair of them to wear to school starting the next day. Just one pair.

There were many clogs of many colors.

A black pair,

      two blue pairs,

  three yellow pairs,

         four red pairs,

   five white pairs,

and many, many more than that. All were ranged in order on wooden stands under the light. Behind the stands, there were other shelves with other pairs of wooden clogs. The blue would be nice when I wear my blue dress, I thought, but the yellow ones would also be nice.

"Which pair would you like, little girl?" asked the lady of the store.

Red?

Blue?

Yellow?

I wondered for a long while. My mother was looking at me, smiling quietly. I thought and thought, and finally decided to take the red ones. They were painted with clear red lacquer, and there was a thong of red and black on each clog.

It was almost dark when we went out of the shop with the new clogs in my hands. Lights were on in the stores, and the goods of the stores looked very pretty under the lights. Polished apples looked as if they were painted.

Fresh bluish fishes looked almost alive on blocks of
shining ice, and roses were still wearing dew on their
dark red petals as if they had just come from the gardens.
But my new clogs were the most beautiful of all!

They were so gay and so light that I felt as if I was
wearing nothing. When I walked, they talked:

KARA KORO, KARA KORO.

When I ran, they sang:

KORO KORO, KARA KARA

along with me. I went to school, I played with my
friends, I went shopping with my mother, wearing the
new pair. Everybody said, "Aren't they pretty!" I was
happy, very happy.

One evening when the sun was going down, my friends and I were walking down the hill. The sun was just setting, and everything looked orange in its rays, the sky, the grasses, my friends, and I. . . . "*Ashita tenkini nare!*" one of the girls sang, and kicked her wooden clogs into the air. "*Ashita tenkini nare!*" (May it be fine tomorrow! it means.) I did it too.

This game is called the weather-telling game, and if your clogs fall to the ground like this,

 it will be a fine day tomorrow.

And if like this,  there will be snow.

And if like this, it will rain.

And that is how I made a crack in my new clogs.

They did not talk:

    KARA KORO, KARA KORO,

when I walked.

They did not sing:

    KORO KORO, KARA KARA,

when I ran.

They just sounded:

    GARA GARA, GORO GORO.

I was . . . sad.

    Shall I ask Mother to buy a new pair? I thought. No, I knew she would not buy another pair so soon. I remembered what she had told me when we bought them. "Take good care of them," she had said. "Maybe I will buy another pair after a while, for the next festival day."

    Oh, it was more than two months till then. "She will not buy new ones yet," I said to myself. So I kept on wearing them. They were not new any more now that there was a crack in them. Day by day, little by little, they got dirtier. Do I have to wear them for another two months? I thought miserably.

    I thought and thought . . . and I had a bright idea! Suppose . . . Suppose this pair got very, very dirty; then Mother could not help buying a new pair, because she wouldn't like me to look dirty among the others.

Let's make this pair very dirty, I decided. The very next day, on my way home from school, I walked into a puddle to get the wooden clogs wet. Then I went to a dusty field and shuffled my feet in the dirt.

Look what I was wearing! Just muddy pieces of wood! "Now Mother must buy me a new pair," I said, "and they will sing

KARA KORO, KARA KORO, when I walk,
KORO KORO, KARA KARA, when I run.

People will say, 'Aren't they pretty?' again." I was very pleased with my plan, and started toward home.

But while I was walking along, scuffing the dirty clogs, I began to get uneasy. I began to be afraid that my

mother would know that I had
made the clogs dirty on purpose.

BETA BETA, BETA BETA,
the muddy pair seemed to
murmur, as if they were saying,
     "You are a liar;
     you are telling a lie."
So, I was walking slowly when
I entered the kitchen where
Mother was cooking. "What's
wrong with you, Mako?" she said, looking at my dirty
feet. "With whom were you playing? The boys? Is that
brown stuff just mud, or is it paint?"

"Just mud," I answered in a low voice.

23 ❧

"Go and wash your clogs quickly before the thongs turn brown. Then squeeze the thongs softly, and wipe the water away with the old washcloth, and put them near the bath-fire. Not too near, otherwise the lacquer will come off," Mother said in her usual soft voice. I didn't move. "What's the matter, Mako? Do it quickly, or they won't dry before morning."

I, I could not say that the clogs were so dirty that I needed a new pair. Mother was not suspecting me at all. And I remembered that you should try to clean a thing first before you decide to buy a new one. It was the way we always did.

So, I washed the clogs. The mud came out easily because it had not yet had time to dry hard.

Splash, splash, splash!

The water was cold, and I was cold too. I was sure that Mother would not buy me a new pair of clogs, because the mud came out almost perfectly.

I squeezed the clog-thongs, and wiped the water away.

Then I put the clogs near the bath-fire, but not too near.
Now that they were clean again they looked quite
pretty, though there was still the crack. And I saw that
the black color of the thongs had come out and dyed
the red part. All because they got wet!

"Come and eat, Mako, it's getting late," called
Mother. So I went and ate, leaving my wooden clogs,
steaming a bit, near the bath-fire in the kitchen. "They
will be dry soon," said Mother.

"Did you wash them by yourself, Mako?" asked Father. "Good, very good."

"What did you play, Mako?" asked my brother curiously.

"I . . . I just played. . . ." I answered in a little, little voice. Now it was out of the question to ask for a new pair. I felt very sad. I was ashamed of what I had done.

"Maybe I will buy a new pair before long," said Mother. "The crack makes too much noise when you run. But don't play the weather-telling game on the stone road, and be sure not to get wooden clogs wet too often. All right, Mako?"

"All right," I said, nodding. Mother was smiling at me as usual, so I tried to smile as usual, too, but I couldn't. I wanted to say something to her . . . but I couldn't. I just knew that I would never try to trick my mother again.

A long, long time has passed since then.

This pair of cracked clogs is almost as old as I am.

I am packing the new pair for my granddaughter.

Will she play the weather-telling game with this pair of clogs?

Will she kick them into the air and let them fall on the stone road?

Will she get them wet?

Yes, I think so, don't you?

27

MEET MASAKO MATSUNO, AUTHOR

Masako Matsuno was born in Japan. She saw her first American picture book when she was in college and decided to come to the United States to study more about children's books and libraries.

Matsuno got her idea for writing A Pair of Red Clogs *one day as she was walking. She began wondering how wooden clogs would sound on the smooth, paved road. Matsuno wondered also how American children would like the clatter of the shoes. "Then I got an idea, or rather, I should say, a wish to tell a story about real Japanese children to American children."*

THE PUDDING LIKE A NIGHT ON THE SEA

Ann Cameron
illustrated by Ann Strugnell

"I'm going to make something special for your mother," my father said.

My mother was out shopping. My father was in the kitchen, looking at the pots and the pans and the jars of this and that.

"What are you going to make?" I said.

"A pudding," he said.

My father is a big man with wild black hair. When he laughs, the sun laughs in the windowpanes. When he thinks, you can almost see his thoughts sitting on all the tables and chairs. When he is angry, me and my little brother Huey shiver to the bottom of our shoes.

"What kind of pudding will you make?" Huey said.

"A wonderful pudding," my father said. "It will taste like a whole raft of lemons. It will taste like a night on the sea."

Then he took down a knife and sliced five lemons in half. He squeezed the first one. Juice squirted in my eye.

"Stand back!" he said, and squeezed again. The seeds flew out on the floor. "Pick up those seeds, Huey!" he said.

Huey took the broom and swept them up.

My father cracked some eggs and put the yolks in a pan and the whites in a bowl. He rolled up his sleeves and pushed back his hair and beat up the yolks. "Sugar, Julian!" he said, and I poured in the sugar.

He went on beating. Then he put in lemon juice and cream and set the pan on the stove. The pudding bubbled and he stirred it fast. Cream splashed on the stove.

"Wipe that up, Huey!" he said.

Huey did.

It was hot by the stove. My father loosened his collar and pushed at his sleeves. The stuff in the pan was getting thicker and thicker. He held the beater up high in the air. "Just right!" he said, and sniffed in the smell of the pudding.

He whipped the egg whites and mixed them into the pudding. The pudding looked softer and lighter than air.

"Done!" he said. He washed all the pots, splashing water on the floor, and wiped the counter so fast his hair made circles around his head.

"Perfect!" he said. "Now I'm going to take a nap. If something important happens, bother me. If nothing important happens, don't bother me. And—the pudding is for your mother. Leave the pudding alone!"

He went to the living room and was asleep in a minute, sitting straight up in his chair.

Huey and I guarded the pudding.

"Oh, it's a wonderful pudding," Huey said.

"With waves on the top like the ocean," I said.

"I wonder how it tastes," Huey said.

"Leave the pudding alone," I said.

"If I just put my finger in—there—I'll know how it tastes," Huey said.

And he did it.

"You did it!" I said. "How does it taste?"

"It tastes like a whole raft of lemons," he said. "It tastes like a night on the sea."

"You've made a hole in the pudding!" I said. "But since you did it, I'll have a taste." And it tasted like a whole night of lemons. It tasted like floating at sea.

"It's such a big pudding," Huey said. "It can't hurt to have a little more."

"Since you took more, I'll have more," I said.

"That was a bigger lick than I took!" Huey said. "I'm going to have more again."

"Whoops!" I said.

"You put in your whole hand!" Huey said. "Look at the pudding you spilled on the floor!"

"I am going to clean it up," I said. And I took the rag from the sink.

"That's not really clean," Huey said.

"It's the best I can do," I said.

"Look at the pudding!" Huey said.

It looked like craters on the moon. "We have to smooth this over," I said. "So it looks the way it did before! Let's get spoons."

And we evened the top of the pudding with spoons, and while we evened it, we ate some more.

"There isn't much left," I said.

"We were supposed to leave the pudding alone," Huey said.

"We'd better get away from here," I said. We ran into our bedroom and crawled under the bed. After a long time we heard my father's voice.

"Come into the kitchen, dear," he said. "I have something for you."

"Why, what is it?" my mother said, out in the kitchen.

Under the bed, Huey and I pressed ourselves to the wall.

"Look," said my father, out in the kitchen. "A wonderful pudding."

"Where is the pudding?" my mother said.

"WHERE ARE YOU BOYS?" my father said. His voice went through every crack and corner of the house.

We felt like two leaves in a storm.

"WHERE ARE YOU? I SAID!" My father's voice was booming.

Huey whispered to me, "I'm scared."

We heard my father walking slowly through the rooms.

"Huey!" he called. "Julian!"

We could see his feet. He was coming into our room.

He lifted the bedspread. There was his face, and his eyes like black lightning. He grabbed us by the legs and pulled. "STAND UP!" he said.

We stood.

"What do you have to tell me?" he said.

"We went outside," Huey said, "and when we came back, the pudding was gone!"

"Then why were you hiding under the bed?" my father said.

We didn't say anything. We looked at the floor.

"I can tell you one thing," he said. "There is going to be some beating here now! There is going to be some whipping!"

The curtains at the window were shaking. Huey was holding my hand.

"Go into the kitchen!" my father said. "Right now!"

We went into the kitchen.

"Come here, Huey!" my father said.

Huey walked toward him, his hands behind his back.

"See these eggs?" my father said. He cracked them and put the yolks in a pan and set the pan on the counter. He stood a chair by the counter. "Stand up here," he said to Huey.

Huey stood on the chair by the counter.

"Now it's time for your beating!" my father said.

Huey started to cry. His tears fell in with the egg yolks.

"Take this!" my father said. My father handed him the egg beater. "Now beat those eggs," he said. "I want this to be a good beating!"

"Oh!" Huey said. He stopped crying. And he beat the egg yolks.

"Now you, Julian, stand here!" my father said.

I stood on a chair by the table.

"I hope you're ready for your whipping!"

I didn't answer. I was afraid to say yes or no.

"Here!" he said, and he set the egg whites in front of me. "I want these whipped and whipped well!"

"Yes, sir!" I said, and started whipping.

My father watched us. My mother came into the kitchen and watched us.

After a while Huey said, "This is hard work."

"That's too bad," my father said. "Your beating's not done!" And he added sugar and cream and lemon juice to Huey's pan and put the pan on the stove. And Huey went on beating.

"My arm hurts from whipping," I said.

"That's too bad," my father said. "Your whipping's not done."

So I whipped and whipped, and Huey beat and beat.

"Hold that beater in the air, Huey!" my father said.

Huey held it in the air.

"See!" my father said. "A good pudding stays on the beater. It's thick enough now. Your beating's done." Then he turned to me. "Let's see those egg whites, Julian!" he said. They were puffed up and fluffy. "Congratulations, Julian!" he said. "Your whipping's done."

He mixed the egg whites into the pudding himself. Then he passed the pudding to my mother.

"A wonderful pudding," she said. "Would you like some, boys?"

"No thank you," we said.

She picked up a spoon. "Why, this tastes like a whole raft of lemons," she said. "This tastes like a night on the sea."

MEET ANN CAMERON, AUTHOR

A friend of Ann Cameron once told her some stories about his childhood. That gave Cameron the idea to write The Stories Julian Tells. *"What started me on the book was his tale of having eaten a pudding his father told him not to eat, since it was being saved for supper."*

That story reminded Cameron that sometimes it was hard for her to obey rules as a child, and to face the consequences if she didn't. Cameron wanted to write the book because she knew that we all have experiences like hers and Julian's.

THE BOY WHO CRIED WOLF

Aesop
retold by Margaret Clark
iIllustrated by Charlotte Voake

A boy was sent to look after a flock of sheep as they grazed near a village. It was raining, and he was bored, so he decided to play a trick on the villagers. "Wolf! Wolf!" he shouted as loud as he could. "There's a wolf attacking your sheep."

Out ran all the villagers, leaving whatever they were doing, to drive away the wolf. When they rushed into the field and found the sheep quite safe, the boy laughed and laughed. The next day the same thing happened.

"Wolf! Wolf!" shouted the boy. And when the villagers ran into the field and again found everything quiet, he laughed more than ever.

On the third day a wolf really did come.

"Wolf! Wolf!" shouted the boy, as the sheep ran wildly in all directions. "Oh, please come quickly!"

But this time the villagers ignored him, because they thought he was only playing tricks, as he had done before. And can you guess what happened next?

THE TALE OF PETER RABBIT

Beatrix Potter

O nce upon a time there
were four little Rabbits,
and their names were—
Flopsy, Mopsy, Cotton-tail, and Peter.
They lived with their mother in a
sand-bank, underneath the root of a
very big fir-tree.

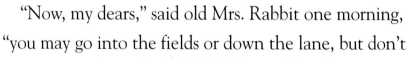

"Now, my dears," said old Mrs. Rabbit one morning,
"you may go into the fields or down the lane, but don't
go into Mr. McGregor's garden: your
Father had an accident there; he was
put in a pie by Mrs. McGregor.

"Now run along, and don't get into mischief. I am going out."

Then old Mrs. Rabbit took a basket and her umbrella, and went through the wood to the baker's. She bought a loaf of brown bread and five currant buns.

41 ❦

Flopsy, Mopsy, and Cotton-tail, who were good little bunnies, went down the lane to gather blackberries.

But Peter, who was very naughty, ran straight away to Mr. McGregor's garden, and squeezed under the gate!

First he ate some lettuces and some French beans; and then he ate some radishes.

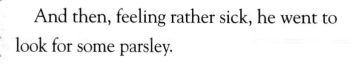

And then, feeling rather sick, he went to look for some parsley.

But round the end of a cucumber frame,
whom should he meet but Mr. McGregor!

Mr. McGregor was on his hands and
knees planting out young cabbages, but
he jumped up and ran after Peter, waving
a rake and calling out, "Stop thief!"

43

Peter was most dreadfully frightened;
he rushed all over the garden, for he had
forgotten the way back to the gate.

He lost one of his shoes among the
cabbages, and the other shoe amongst the
potatoes.

After losing them, he ran on four legs and went faster, so that I think he might have got away altogether if he had not unfortunately run into a gooseberry net, and got caught by the large buttons on his jacket.

It was a blue jacket with brass buttons, quite new.

Peter gave himself up for lost, and shed big tears; but his sobs were overheard by some friendly sparrows, who flew to him in great excitement, and implored him to exert himself.

Mr. McGregor came up with a sieve, which he intended to pop upon the top of Peter; but Peter wriggled out just in time, leaving his jacket behind him.

And rushed into the tool-shed, and jumped into a can. It would have been a beautiful thing to hide in, if it had not had so much water in it.

Mr. McGregor was quite sure that Peter was somewhere in the tool-shed, perhaps hidden underneath a flower-pot. He began to turn them over carefully, looking under each.

Presently Peter sneezed—"Kertyschoo!" Mr. McGregor was after him in no time.

45

And tried to put his foot upon Peter, who jumped out of a window, upsetting three plants. The window was too small for Mr. McGregor, and he was tired of running after Peter. He went back to his work.

Peter sat down to rest; he was out of breath and trembling with fright, and he had not the least idea which way to go. Also he was very damp with sitting in that can.

After a time he began to wander about, going lippity—lippity—not very fast, and looking all round.

He found a door in a wall; but it was locked, and there was no room for a fat little rabbit to squeeze underneath.

An old mouse was running in and out over the stone door-step, carrying peas and beans to her family in the wood. Peter asked her the way to the gate, but she had such a large pea in her mouth that she could not answer. She only shook her head at him. Peter began to cry.

Then he tried to find his way straight across the garden, but he became more and more puzzled. Presently, he came to a pond where Mr. McGregor filled his water-cans. A white cat was staring at some goldfish, she sat very, very still, but now and then the tip of her tail twitched as if it were alive. Peter thought

it best to go away without speaking to her;
he had heard about cats from his cousin,
little Benjamin Bunny.

He went back towards the
tool-shed, but suddenly, quite close
to him, he heard the noise of a
hoe—scr-r-ritch, scratch, scratch,
scritch. Peter scuttered underneath
the bushes. But presently, as nothing
happened, he came out, and climbed
upon a wheelbarrow and peeped
over. The first thing he saw was Mr.
McGregor hoeing onions. His back
was turned towards Peter, and
beyond him was the gate!

47 ❧

Peter got down very quietly off the
wheelbarrow, and started running as fast as
he could go, along a straight walk behind
some black-currant bushes.

Mr. McGregor caught sight of him at the
corner, but Peter did not care. He slipped
underneath the gate, and was safe at last in
the wood outside the garden.

Mr. McGregor hung up the little jacket and the shoes for a scarecrow to frighten the blackbirds.

Peter never stopped running or looked behind him till he got home to the big fir-tree.

He was so tired that he flopped down upon the nice soft sand on the floor of the rabbit-hole and shut his eyes. His mother was busy cooking; she wondered what he had done with his clothes. It was the second little jacket and pair of shoes that Peter had lost in a fortnight!

I am sorry to say that Peter was not very well during the evening.

His mother put him to bed, and made some camomile tea; and she gave a dose of it to Peter!

"One tablespoonful to be taken at bed-time."

But Flopsy, Mopsy, and Cotton-tail had bread and milk and blackberries for supper.

49

MEET BEATRIX POTTER, AUTHOR

Beatrix Potter was born in 1866 in London, England. The Tale of Peter Rabbit was originally a letter with pictures that Potter, then 27 years old, sent to the young son of her governess, or private teacher, to entertain him while he was ill. The letter began: "I don't know what to write to you, so I shall tell you the story about four little rabbits, whose names were Flopsy, Mopsy, Cotton-tail, and Peter."

During the years that followed, Potter sent many more picture letters to the children of the governess. She learned how much they loved the letters, and this probably gave her the idea of writing books for children.

50

Rocking Chair #1. Edition of 6. 1950. Henry Moore.

Bronze. Photo: SCALA/Art Resource

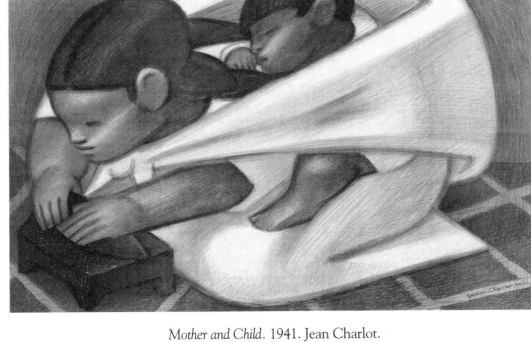

Mother and Child. 1941. Jean Charlot.

Lithograph, printed in color, composition, 12 1/2" x 18 5/8". Gift of Albert Carman,
The Museum of Modern Art, New York

Unfaithful Shepherd. Before 1600. Attributed to Marten van Cleve
after a composition by Pieter Bruegel the Elder.

Oil on panel. The John G. Johnson Collection, Philadelphia Museum of Art

THREE HUNDRED SPARTANS

Sonia Bradoz
illustrated by Rebecca Guay

Long ago, when mighty kings ruled in the world, the lands of Greece and Persia were at war. The king of Persia ruled over a huge land called the Persian Empire. He had land and sea armies of over five million men. Now the king wanted to rule over Greece, too. The great king had sent messengers into every Greek city-state, asking for a jug of water and a clump of earth. He wanted these things as proof that he would soon own the Greek land and sea. The Greeks sent back their answer, "Never! We shall be free!"

So the king of Persia and his huge army marched toward Greece to fight the Greeks. The Greeks prepared to defend their homeland. They armed themselves with arrows, shields, and spears.

There was only one way for the Persian army to enter Greece. It was by a narrow pass in the mountains, in a place called Thermopylae. The pass was only fifty feet wide. In this small place, the large size of the Persian army would make little difference. Only a handful of Persian soldiers could enter the pass at one time. Here the Greeks thought they could meet and stop their enemy from entering into Greece.

Each Greek city-state had its own army, led by a general. The most respected general was Leonidas, king of the Greek city-state called Sparta. He was ordered to defend the pass. Leonidas had an army of only three hundred Spartans. The other generals promised him that some of their soldiers would join him soon.

Leonidas and his men marched on toward the pass. On their way, a few thousand Greeks from different city-states joined the little army, but it was still a little army compared to the great numbers of Persian soldiers. Soon, Leonidas and his men reached the pass. They camped there and waited to do battle with the Persians.

The Persian king and his soldiers marched on from the north and camped about five miles from Thermopylae. The king sent a scout to see how many Greeks were waiting for him. When he was told there were only a few thousand, he waited for four days. Surely, the Greeks would be afraid of the size of his mighty army. They would run away. But the Greeks did not move. On the fourth day, one of the king's advisors told him, "These men are Spartans. They have come to the pass to do battle with us. You are now face-to-face with the bravest men in Greece." But the Persian king did not believe him. He waited one more day.

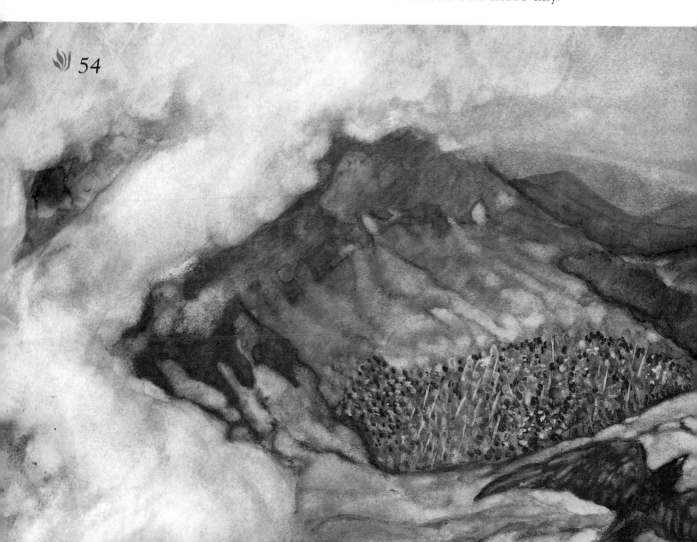

Finally, on the fifth day, the king sent soldiers to capture the Spartans and bring them to him. For two days his soldiers fought hand-to-hand with the Spartans. The Spartans fought bravely. They proved that they were better soldiers than the Persians. By the second day, the Spartans had pushed the Persians back to their camp.

That night, a Greek traitor offered to show the Persian king a secret path. It led over the top of the mountain and behind the Greeks defending the pass.

That very same night, the Persians started marching up the mountain. At sunrise they reached the top.

There, they met a thousand Greek soldiers. They had promised Leonidas they would defend that side of the mountain. But the Persian army was too big for the Greeks to fight. The Greeks found themselves showered with a heavy rain of arrows. Soon they were defeated.

Greek lookouts ran down the mountain to warn Leonidas that the Persians were coming from that side. There were so many Persian soldiers, the lookouts said, that when they shot their arrows, the arrows blocked the sun. A Spartan answered, "Then we shall fight them in the shade!"

Leonidas knew that all his men would surely die in the battle to come. The Persians were too many for his small army to fight them and win. He also knew that he could not leave. He was responsible for defending the pass. He stood in front of his soldiers and told them they could not win this battle. Then he ordered all those who wanted to leave to do so. He would stay and carry out his orders. Only the Spartans chose to stay with him. Leonidas was their general. They knew it was their duty to fight the Persians, even if it meant their death.

So Leonidas and his Spartans met the Persian soldiers outside the narrow gates. They fought in the wider part of the pass. In time, most of the Spartans had broken their spears. Then they fought with their swords, their fists, and their teeth. Such was the bravery of the Spartans. Leonidas was killed in the battle. He showed himself to be the bravest of all. Before the day was over, there were no Spartans left.

Leonidas and his three hundred Spartans were buried in Thermopylae, where they were killed defending their country. There the Greeks placed an inscription in their honor. It says:

Stranger passing by, go tell the Spartans
that here we obeyed orders, and here we fell.

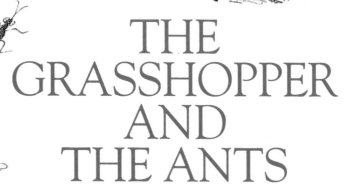

THE GRASSHOPPER AND THE ANTS

Aesop
retold by Margaret Clark
illustrated by *Charlotte Voake*

58

One winter's day, when the sun came out unexpectedly, all the ants hurried out of their anthill and began to spread out their store of grain to dry.

Up came a grasshopper who said, "I'm so hungry. Please will you give me some of your grain?"

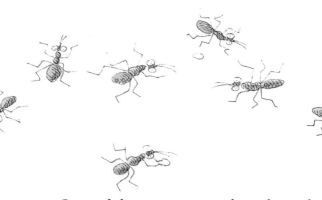

One of the ants stopped working for a moment and replied, "Why should we? What's happened to your own store of food for the winter?"

"I haven't got a store," said the grasshopper. "I didn't have time to collect any food last summer because I spent the whole time singing."

The ant laughed and all the others joined in. "If you spent the summer singing, you'll have to spend the winter dancing for your supper."

And the grasshopper went on his way, hungry.

59 ❧

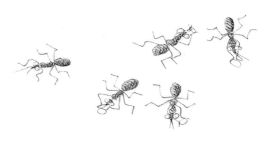

BIBLIOGRAPHY

Anatole and the Cat by Eve Titus. Anatole the mouse works hard as taste-tester in the cheese factory, but . . . how is he going to deal with a cat in his place of work? Read this wonderful story and find out how Anatole solves his problem.

The Comeback Dog by Jane Resh Thomas. A boy takes on a big job; he wants to nurse a stray dog back to health. Can he do it?

The Girl Who Knew It All by Patricia Reilly Giff. Tracy lets a number of responsibilities slip away from her. How will she take care of the problems that follow?

Henry and the Paper Route by Beverly Cleary. Go along with Henry on his paper route. How he handles this responsibility may surprise you!

Jamaica's Find by Juanita Havill. Jamaica finds a stuffed toy in the park. She likes the toy very much and decides to keep it. Then she finds out who the owner is. Will she return the toy?

M & M and the Big Bag by Pat Ross. Read about two girls who go to the grocery store for the first time and have to make their own decisions about how to spend the money.

Strega Nona retold by Tomie dePaola. This delightful story tells about Big Anthony, who becomes Strega Nona's assistant. She tells him he must not touch a magic pot while she is out. Of course, he touches it anyway—with terrible consequences.

The Sunflower Garden by Janice May Udry. Discover how an Algonkian girl takes care of all her tribal responsibilities and then adds a new one, finally earning the respect of her father and brothers.

61

62

APPEARANCES

63

CROW BOY
Taro Yashima

On the first day of our village school in Japan,
there was a boy missing. He was found
hidden away in the dark space underneath
the schoolhouse floor. None of us knew him. He was
nicknamed Chibi because he was very small. Chibi
means "tiny boy."

This strange boy was afraid of our teacher and could
not learn a thing. He was afraid of the children and
could not make friends with them at all.

He was left alone in the study time. He was left alone in the play time. He was always at the end of the line, always at the foot of the class, a forlorn little tag-along.

Soon Chibi began to make his eyes cross-eyed, so that he was able not to see whatever he did not want to see.

And Chibi found many ways, one after another, to kill time and amuse himself.

Just the ceiling was interesting enough for him to watch for hours. The wooden top of his desk was another thing interesting to watch. A patch of cloth on a boy's shoulder was something to study. Of course the window showed him many things all year round. Even when it was raining the window had surprising things to show him.

On the playground, if he closed his eyes and listened, Chibi could hear many different sounds, near and far. And Chibi could hold and watch insects and grubs that most of us wouldn't touch or even look at—so that not only the children in our class but the older ones and even the younger ones called him stupid and slowpoke.

But, slowpoke or not, day after day Chibi came trudging to school. He always carried the same lunch, a rice ball wrapped in a radish leaf. Even when it rained or stormed he still came trudging along, wrapped in a raincoat made from dried zebra grass.

And so, day by day, five years went by, and we were in the sixth grade, the last class in school. Our new teacher was Mr. Isobe. He was a friendly man with a kind smile.

Mr. Isobe often took his class to the hilltop behind the school. He was pleased to learn that Chibi knew all the places where the wild grapes and wild potatoes grew. He was amazed to find how much Chibi knew about all the flowers in our class garden.

He liked Chibi's black-and-white drawings and tacked them up on the wall to be admired. He liked Chibi's own handwriting, which no one but Chibi could read, and he tacked that up on the wall. And he often spent time talking with Chibi when no one was around.

But, when Chibi appeared on the stage at the
talent show of that year, no one could believe his eyes.
"Who is that?" "What can that stupid do up there?"
Until Mr. Isobe announced that Chibi was going to
imitate the voices of crows. "Voices?" "Voices of
crows?" "Voices of *crows!*"

"VOICES OF CROWS."

First he imitated the voices of newly hatched
crows. And he made the mother crow's voice.
Then he imitated the father
crow's voice. He showed how
crows cry early in the morning. He showed
how crows cry when the village people have some
unhappy accident. He showed how crows call when
they are happy and gay. Everybody's mind was taken
to the far mountainside from which Chibi
probably came to the school.

At the end, to imitate a crow on an old tree, Chibi
made very special sounds deep down in his throat.
"KAUUWWATT! KAUUWWATT!" Now everybody
could imagine exactly the far and lonely place where
Chibi lived with his family.

Then Mr. Isobe explained how Chibi had
learned those calls—leaving his home for
school at dawn, and arriving home at sunset,
every day for six long years. Every one of us
cried, thinking how much we had been
wrong to Chibi all those long years.

Even grownups wiped their eyes, saying,
"Yes, yes, he is wonderful."

Soon after that came graduation day. Chibi was the only one in our class honored for perfect attendance through all the six years.

After school was over, the big boys would often have work to do in the village for their families. Sometimes Chibi came to the village to sell the charcoal he and his family made. But nobody called him Chibi any more. We all called him Crow Boy. "Hi, Crow Boy!"

Crow Boy would nod and smile as if he liked the name. And when his work was done he would buy a few things for his family. Then he would set off for his home on the far side of the mountain, stretching his growing shoulders proudly like a grown-up man. And from around the turn of the mountain road would come a crow call—the happy one.

MEET TARO YASHIMA, AUTHOR AND ILLUSTRATOR

Taro Yashima was born in Japan and came to the United States when he was thirty years old. He began writing children's books to explain to his daughter what life was like for him as a boy in Japan. He wants his books to be more than interesting stories about Japan, though. He wants to let children know, wherever they are, that they can enjoy life and be strong enough to do what is right.

THE FOOLISH, TIMID RABBIT

retold by Ellen C. Babbitt
illustrated by Hilary Knight

Once upon a time, a Rabbit was asleep under a palm tree. All at once he woke up, and thought: "What if the world should break up! What then would become of me?"

At that moment, some Monkeys dropped a coconut. It fell down on the ground just back of the Rabbit.

Hearing the noise, the Rabbit said to himself: "The earth is all breaking up!"

72

And he jumped up and ran just as fast as he could, without even looking back to see what made the noise.

Another Rabbit saw him running, and called after him, "What are you running so fast for?"

"Don't ask me!" he cried.

But the other Rabbit ran after him, begging to know what was the matter.

Then the first Rabbit said: "Don't you know? The earth is all breaking up!"

And on he ran, and the second Rabbit ran with him.

The next Rabbit they met ran with them when he heard that the earth was all breaking up.

One Rabbit after another joined them, until there were hundreds of Rabbits running as fast as they could go.

73

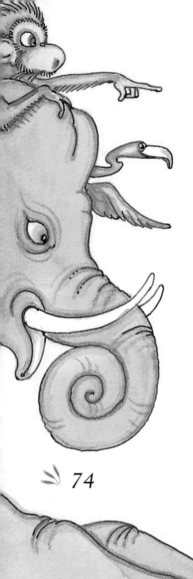

They passed a Deer, calling out to him that the earth was all breaking up. The Deer then ran with them.

The Deer called to a Fox to come along because the earth was all breaking up.

On and on they ran, and an Elephant joined them.

At last the Lion saw the animals running, and heard their cry that the earth was all breaking up.

He thought there must be some mistake, so he ran to the foot of a hill in front of them and roared three times.

This stopped them, for they knew the voice of the King of Beasts, and they feared him.

"Why are you running so fast?" asked the Lion.

"Oh, King Lion," they answered him, "the earth is all breaking up!"

"Who saw it breaking up?" asked the Lion.

"I didn't," said the Elephant. "Ask the Fox—he told me about it."

"I didn't," said the Fox.

"The Rabbits told me about it," said the Deer.

One after another of the Rabbits said: "I did not see it, but another Rabbit told me about it."

At last the Lion came to the Rabbit who had first said the earth was all breaking up.

"Is it true that the earth is all breaking up?" the Lion asked.

"Yes, O Lion, it is," said the Rabbit. "I was asleep under a palm tree. I woke up and thought, 'What would become of me if the earth should all break up?' At that very moment, I heard the sound of the earth breaking up, and I ran away."

"Then," said the Lion, "you and I will go back to the place where the earth began to break up, and see what is the matter."

So the Lion put the little Rabbit on his back, and away they went like the wind. The other animals waited for them at the foot of the hill.

The Rabbit told the Lion when they were near the place where he slept, and the Lion saw just where the Rabbit had been sleeping.

He saw, too, the coconut that had fallen to the ground near by. Then the Lion said to the Rabbit, "It must have been the sound of the coconut falling to the ground that you heard. You foolish Rabbit!"

And the Lion ran back to the other animals, and told them all about it.

If it had not been for the wise King of Beasts, they might be running still.

HOW WE LEARNED THE EARTH IS ROUND

Patricia Lauber

illustrated by Megan Lloyd

Today nearly everybody knows that the earth is round.

But long ago, people were sure the earth was flat. They thought it was flat because it looked flat. It still does.

Stand out on the prairie. Sail out onto the ocean. You can see for miles, and the earth looks flat.

Climb a mountain. Now the earth looks rough and
bumpy, but it doesn't seem to curve. It doesn't look round.

The earth looks flat because it is big and we are small.
We see only a tiny piece at one time. The tiny piece does
curve, but the curve is too slight for our eyes to see. And
that is why, for thousands of years, people thought the
earth was flat.

The earth's real shape was discovered about 2,500 years
ago. The people who discovered it were Greeks.

At first the Greeks, too, believed the earth was flat. But
certain Greeks were great thinkers. They thought hard
about things they saw and tried to explain them. They
asked themselves questions—Why? What if? And then
they thought some more.

Everybody knew that a strange thing happened when a ship left harbor. As it sailed away, it appeared to sink. First the hull disappeared, then the bottom of the sail, then the top.

As a ship returned, it seemed to rise out of the sea. First the sail appeared, then the hull.

The Greeks wondered why.

Why didn't the whole ship just get smaller and smaller or bigger and bigger? That's what should happen on a flat earth.

But it didn't happen. Why didn't it?

Perhaps the answer had to do with the shape of the earth. Perhaps the earth wasn't flat after all. Perhaps it had some other shape.

What if the earth had a curved surface? What would happen to a ship then?

You can see what happens yourself. Use a big ball and a ship made from an eraser, a toothpick, and a piece of paper. With one hand, hold the ball in front of you at eye level. Use the other hand to move the ship.

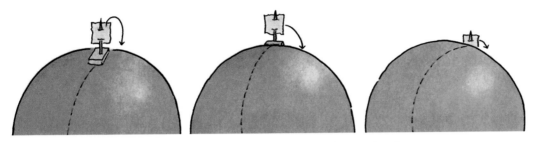

When a ship sails away over a curved surface, the bottom disappears first. When it returns, the top appears first.

The Greeks decided the earth must have a curved surface. That would explain why ships seemed to sink and rise.

81

They also saw that the same thing happened no matter which way a ship was heading—east, west, north, or south. The earth must curve in all directions.

Was it round? They found the answer in the night sky.

The Greeks had studied the skies for many years. They knew that the sun made its own light and the moon did not. The moon shone because it reflected light from the sun.

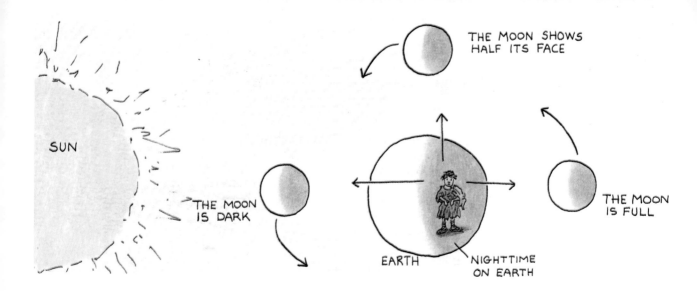

THE MOON SHOWS HALF ITS FACE

SUN

THE MOON IS DARK

THE MOON IS FULL

EARTH

NIGHTTIME ON EARTH

They also knew that the moon traveled around the earth. As it did so, different parts of it were lighted up by the sun. That was why the moon seemed to change its shape, why they might see a sliver of moon, a bigger piece, or a full moon. They saw a full moon whenever the moon was on the far side of the earth from the sun.

But sometimes a shadow dimmed the light of a full moon—an eclipse took place. The shadow seemed to sweep across the face of the moon. The edge of the shadow was curved. It was like part of a circle.

The Greeks knew that this shadow was the earth's. It was the shadow that the earth cast in space. When the moon moved through the shadow, an eclipse took place.

Sometimes the moon was high in the sky during an eclipse. Sometimes it was low. Yet as long as the sun, earth, and moon were lined up, an eclipse took place. And the edge of the shadow was always the same curve.

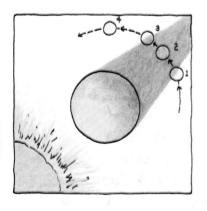

There is only one shape that always casts the same shadow. That shape is round. A ball, for example, always casts the same shadow no matter how it is turned. It casts the same shadow no matter where the light is coming from.

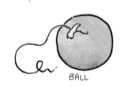

BALL

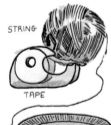

STRING

TAPE

PAPER PLATE

And that is how the Greeks found out the earth is round. You can test the discovery yourself. Shine a bright light on a plate, a can, and a ball. You can make each one cast a circle-shaped shadow on a wall in front of you. But only the ball always casts this shadow.

FLASHLIGHT

Today we have spaceships and satellites in space. They take photos of the earth. People everywhere can see for themselves: The earth is round.

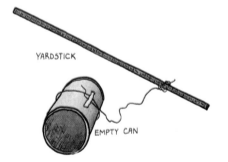

YARDSTICK

EMPTY CAN

MEET PATRICIA LAUBER, AUTHOR

Patricia Lauber says, "Some of my books are fiction, and some are nonfiction, but all are based on what I've seen around me. I like to stand and stare at things, to talk with people, and to read a lot. From this I'm always learning something I didn't know before." When she writes nonfiction, she must do a great deal of research. "One nice thing about being a writer is that sailing a boat or exploring a forest can often be 'doing research,'" Ms. Lauber explains.

THE FOX AND THE CROW

retold by Margaret Clark
illustrated by Charlotte Voake

One day a crow snatched a piece of cheese
from an open cottage window and flew up
into a tree, where she sat on a branch to eat
it. A fox, walking by, saw the crow and at once wanted
the cheese for himself.

"O Crow," he said, "how beautiful your feathers are! And what bright eyes you have. Your wings shine like polished ebony, and your head sparkles like a glistening jewel. If your voice is as sweet as your looks are fair, you must be the queen of the birds."

The unwary crow believed every word, and, to show how sweet her voice was, she opened her mouth to sing. Out dropped the cheese, which the fox instantly gobbled up.

"You may have a voice," he said to the crow as he went on his way, "but whatever happened to your brains?"

85

MEET MARGARET CLARK, AUTHOR

No one knows exactly who Aesop was. Some say he was a slave who lived on a Greek island hundreds of years ago. The stories he told weren't written down by anyone for hundreds of years. Since then, many people have retold his famous fables.

Margaret Clark wanted to rewrite Aesop's fables because she thought that most other authors left out the fun that was originally in the fables. She believed Aesop probably told his stories mostly to entertain people, and she wanted to retell these stories in such a way that children would again enjoy reading them.

WHO HAS SEEN THE WIND?
Christina Rossetti

Who has seen the wind?
        Neither I nor you:
But when the leaves hang trembling,
        The wind is passing through.

Who has seen the wind?
        Neither you nor I:
But when the trees bow down their heads,
        The wind is passing by.

86

illustrated by Jenny Williams

AN EMERALD
IS AS GREEN AS GRASS
Christina Rossetti

An emerald is as green as grass,
    A ruby red as blood.
A sapphire shines as blue as heaven;
    A flint lies in the mud.

A diamond is a brilliant stone,
    To catch the world's desire.
An opal holds a fiery spark;
    But a flint holds fire.

87

WAKING
Lilian Moore

My secret way of waking
is like a place
to hide.
I'm very still,
my eyes are shut.
They all think I am sleeping
but
I'm wide awake inside.

88

They all think I am sleeping
but
I'm wiggling my toes.
I feel sun-fingers
on my cheek.
I hear voices whisper-speak.
I squeeze my eyes
to keep them shut
so they will think I'm sleeping
BUT
I'm really wide awake inside
—and no one knows!

90

Day and Night. 1938.
M.C. Escher.

Woodcut. Gift of Mrs. Herbert C. Morris,
Philadelphia Museum of Art. © 1938 M.C.
Escher Foundation, Baarn, Holland

Round Blue Roofscape. 1986.
Lidya Buzio.

Earthenware, 11.5" x 8.5". Garth Clark
Gallery, New York. Photo: Anthony Cunha

The Blank Signature. 1965.
René Magritte.

Oil on canvas. Collection of Mr. and
Mrs. Paul Mellon, National Gallery of Art,
Smithsonian Institution, Washington D.C.
© 1993 C. Herscovici/ARS, NY.
Photo: © 1993 National Gallery of Art

91

Fisheye view of
buildings. c. 1920–1934.
Man Ray.

Photograph. © 1994 Man Ray Trust,
ADAGP, Paris

THE EMPEROR'S NEW CLOTHES

Hans Christian Andersen
retold and illustrated by Virginia Lee Burton

M any years ago there lived an Emperor. He was so fond of new clothes that he spent all his time and all his money in order to be well dressed.

He did not care about his soldiers nor did he go to the theatre or even ride out except to show off his beautiful new clothes. He had a different suit for every hour of the day.

People would ask, "Where is the Emperor?" Instead of answering, "He is in council with his Ministers," his officers would reply, "The Emperor is changing his clothes in his dressing room."

92

Time passed merrily in the big town which was the Emperor's capital city.

Visitors arrived every day at court and one day there came two men who called themselves weavers, but they were in fact clever robbers.

They pretended that they knew how to weave cloth of the most beautiful colors and magnificent patterns. Moreover, they said, the clothes woven from this magic cloth could not be seen by anyone who was unfit for the office he held or who was very stupid. The beautiful clothes could only be seen by those who were fit for the offices they held or who were very clever.

"These, indeed, must be splendid clothes!" thought the Emperor. "If I had a suit made of this magic cloth, I could find out at once what men in my kingdom are not good enough for the positions they hold, and I should be able to tell who are wise and who are foolish. This stuff must be woven for me immediately." And he ordered large sums of money to be given to both the weavers in order that they might begin their work at once.

So the two men who pretended to be weavers set up two looms and went on as though they were working

very busily, though in reality they did nothing at all. They asked for the most delicate silk and the purest gold thread. This they kept for themselves and put quietly into their knapsacks and then went on with their pretended work at the empty looms until far into the night.

After some little time had passed, the Emperor said to himself, "I should like to know how the weavers are getting along with my cloth. I am a little bit worried about going myself to look at the cloth because they said that a fool or a man unfit for his office would be unable to see the material. I am sure that I am quite safe but all the same I think it best to send someone else first."

All the people throughout the city had already heard of the wonderful cloth and its magic and all were anxious to learn how wise or how stupid their friends and neighbors might be.

"I will send my faithful old Minister to see how the weavers are getting on with my cloth," said the Emperor at last and after some thought. "He will be the best possible person to see how the cloth looks for he is a man of sense, and no one can be more suitable for his office than he is."

So the honest old Minister went into the hall where the wicked men were working with all their might at the empty looms.

"What can be the meaning of this?" thought the old man, opening his eyes very wide. "I cannot see the least bit of thread on the looms nor the least bit of cloth woven!" However, he did not speak his thoughts out loud.

The men who were pretending to weave asked him very politely to be so good as to come nearer, and then, pointing to the empty looms, asked him whether the design pleased him and whether the colors were not very beautiful.

The poor old Minister looked and looked but he could not see anything on the looms for the very good reason that there was nothing there. But, of course, he did not know this and thought only that he must be a foolish man or unfit for the office of Minister.

"Dear me," he said to himself, "I must never tell anyone that I could not see the cloth."

"Well, Sir Minister," said one of the weavers, still pretending to work. "You do not say whether or not the stuff pleases you!"

"Oh! It is most beautiful!" said the Minister quickly, peering at the loom through his spectacles. "This pattern and the colors! Yes, I will tell the Emperor without delay how very wonderful I think them."

"We shall be most grateful to you," said the pretended weavers, and they named the different colors. The old Minister listened closely to their fine words so that he could repeat them to the Emperor, and then the wicked men asked for more silk and gold, saying they needed it to finish what they had begun.

Again they were given costly thread and silk and again they put it all into their knapsacks and went on pretending to work as busily as before.

The Emperor was pleased with the report brought by his Minister and soon after sent another officer of his court to see how the men were getting on and to find out how soon the cloth would be ready.

It was, of course, just the same with the officer as it had been with the Minister. He looked at the looms on all sides, but could see nothing at all but the empty frames.

"Does not the stuff appear as beautiful to you as it did to my Lord the Minister?" asked the men, at the same time pointing to the empty looms and talking of the design and colors that were not there.

"I certainly am not stupid," thought the officer. "It must be that I am not fit for the very good comfortable office I have. That is very odd indeed. However, no one shall ever know anything about it." And at once he turned to the knaves and praised the material he could not see, saying he was delighted with both colors and patterns.

He then returned to the Emperor and said, "Indeed, please your Imperial Majesty, the cloth which the weavers are making is extraordinarily magnificent."

T he whole city was talking about the splendid cloth which the Emperor had ordered to be woven at such great cost.

And now at last the Emperor wished to go himself and see the marvelous cloth while it was still on the loom. He took with him a few of the officers of the court, among whom were the officer and the Minister who had already seen the cloth and come back with tales of its beauty.

As soon as the pretended weavers heard the Emperor coming, they worked away harder than ever, though they still did not weave a single thread through the empty looms.

"Is not the cloth magnificent?" said the officer and the Minister who had already seen the weavers' pretended work. "If your Majesty will only be so good as to look at it! What a splendid design! What glorious colors!" And at the same time they pointed at the empty frames because they thought that everyone else could see the wonderful work of the weavers even if they could not see it themselves.

"How is this?" said the Emperor to himself, "I can see nothing! This is indeed terrible! Am I a stupid man, or am I unfit to be Emperor? That would be the worst thing that could happen."

"Oh! The cloth is beautiful," he cried out loud, "I am delighted with it," and he smiled most charmingly for on no account would he say that he could not see what his officer and Minister had praised so much.

All his followers now strained their eyes hoping to see something in the looms but they could see no more than the others. Nevertheless, they all exclaimed, "Oh, how beautiful!" and advised His Majesty the Emperor to have some new clothes made from this splendid material and to wear them in the great procession that was soon to take place.

"Magnificent! Charming! Excellent!" were said over and over again and everyone was very gay indeed. The Emperor pretended to share in the pleasure of his followers and presented the two rogues with the title of Gentlemen Weavers and the ribbon of an order of Knighthood to be worn in their buttonholes.

The wicked men sat up all night before the day on which the procession was to take place. They had sixteen lights burning so that everyone might see how eager they were to finish the Emperor's new clothes.

They pretended to roll the cloth off the looms. They cut the air with their scissors and sewed with needles without any thread in them. "See!" they cried at last, "The Emperor's new suit is ready!"

And now the Emperor and all his court came to see the weaver's work; and the rogues raised their arms as though they were holding up something to be seen and said, "Here are your Majesty's trousers! Here is the scarf! Here is the coat! The whole suit is as light as a cobweb!"

"When dressed in it one might fancy that one has on nothing at all. That, however, is the wonderful thing about this delicate magic cloth."

"Yes, indeed!" said all the Court although not one of them could see anything at all.

"If your Imperial Majesty would be graciously pleased to take off your clothes, we will fit on the new suit and undergarments in front of the mirror."

The Emperor was then undressed, and the rogues pretended to dress him in his new clothes, the Emperor turning round from side to side in front of the mirror.

"How splendid His Majesty looks in his new clothes! And how well they fit!" everyone cried out. "What a design! What colors! They are indeed royal robes!"

"The canopy which is to be carried over your Majesty in the procession is waiting," now said the Chief Master of Ceremonies.

"I am quite ready," answered the Emperor. "Do my clothes fit well?" asked he, turning himself around again in front of the mirror in order that he might look as though he were admiring his handsome suit.

The Lords of the Bedchamber who were to carry His Majesty's train felt about on the ground as if they were lifting up the ends and then pretended to be carrying something. They could never for a moment let anyone think that they were stupid or unfit for their office.

So now the Emperor walked under his high canopy in the middle of the procession right through the streets of his capital city. And all the people standing by and those at the windows cried out, "Oh, how beautiful are our Emperor's new clothes! What a magnificent train! And how gracefully the scarf hangs!" In fact, no one would admit that he could not see these clothes which everyone seemed to think so beautiful for fear he would be called a simpleton or unfit for his office.

Never before had any of the Emperor's clothes caused so much excitement as these.

"But the Emperor has nothing on at all!!!" said a little child.

"The child tells the truth," said the father. And so it was that what the child said was whispered from one to another until all knew and they cried out altogether, "BUT HE HAS NOTHING ON AT ALL!!!"

The Emperor felt very silly for he knew that the people were right but he thought, "The procession has started and it must go on now!" So the Lords of the Bedchamber held their heads higher than ever and took greater trouble to pretend to hold up the train which wasn't there at all.

BIBLIOGRAPHY

Crafty Chameleon by Mwenye Hadithi and Adrienne Kennaway. Chameleon is always being bullied by Leopard and Crocodile. Then one day he finds a way to get Leopard and Crocodile to leave him alone. How do you think he does this? Read and find out!

Fables by Arnold Lobel. The animals in these stories run into some surprising— and very funny—situations.

The Garden of Abdul Gasazi by Chris Van Allsburg. A magician performs some changes—or does he?

Grandaddy's Place by Helen V. Griffith. Janetta finds everything about grandfather's farm strange and unpleasant. But before long she is pleasantly surprised!

Looking for Henry by Elaine Livermore.
A leopard is sad that he always blends
into his background and never gets
noticed. Finally, he discovers that spots
have their place.

Sam, Bangs & Moonshine
by Evaline Ness. What can happen when
someone doesn't tell the truth? A little
girl learns how dangerous it can be.

Sylvester and the Magic Pebble
by William Steig. A young donkey is
turned into a rock. How can he return to
being a donkey?

Who's Hiding Here? by Yoshi.
This story tells about animal camouflage.
Can you find the animals hiding
throughout the book?

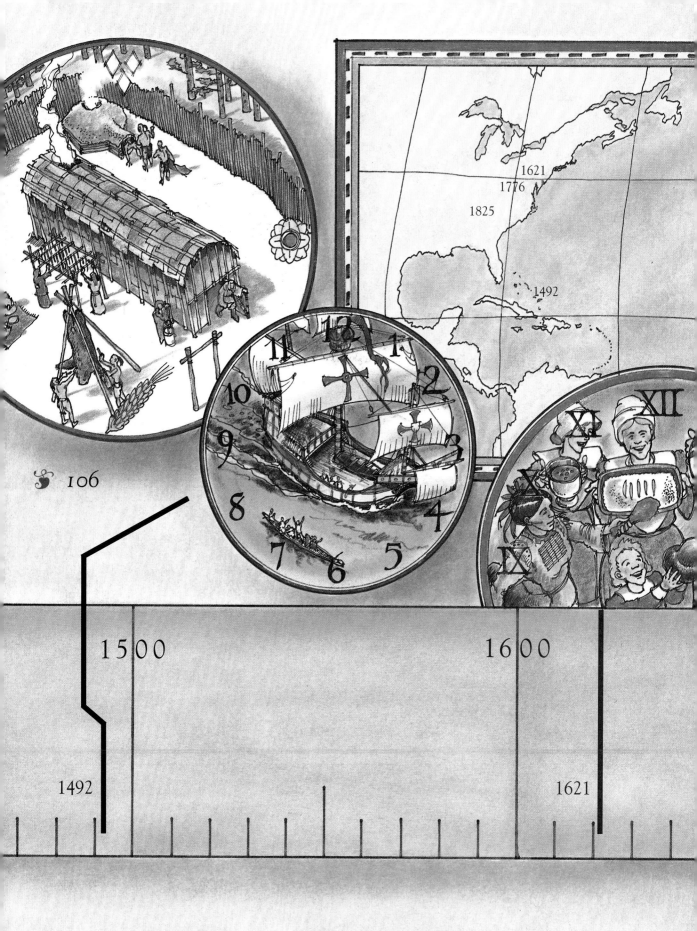

106

1621
1776
1825
1492

1500

1600

1492

1621

OUR COUNTRY: THE EARLY YEARS

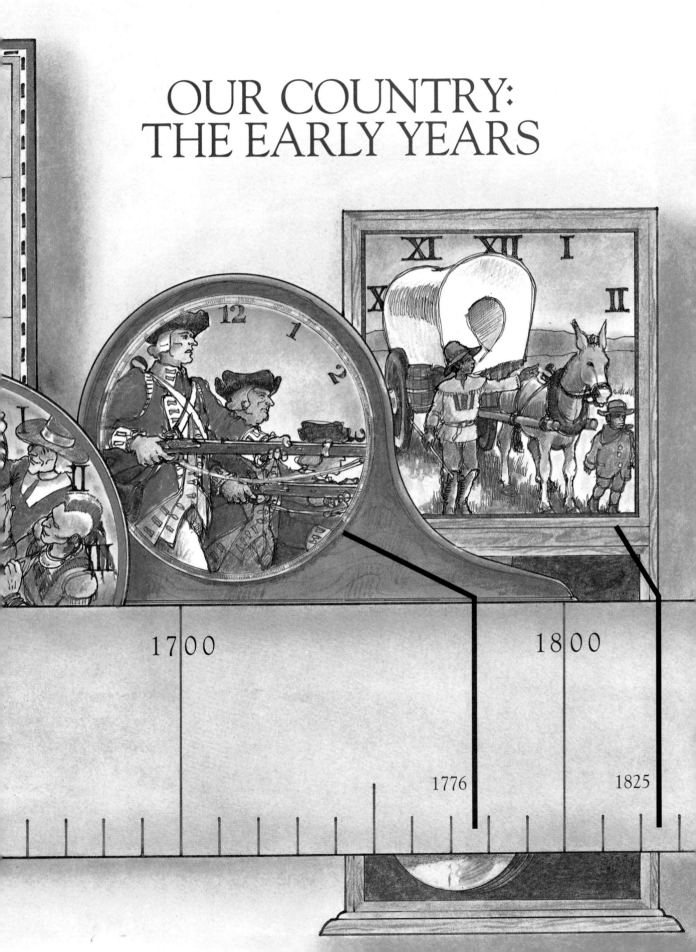

1700

1800

1776

1825

THE FIRST AMERICANS

Jane Werner Watson
illustrated by Troy Howell
landscapes by Jane Kendall

PEOPLE OF THE
PLAINS

108

Long years ago in all our wide land there were no cities. There were no railways or roads. There were no horses or wheels. But there were people living here.

The people lived in small groups scattered over the land. Some wandered across the wide grassy plains hunting for food. They carried their homes—called *tepees*—with them. The women and girls of these groups could set up the tepees quickly.

The men hunted wild buffalo. The people ate the meat of the buffalo. They wore its hide for clothing. They covered their tepees with buffalo hide. The men made tools from buffalo bones. No wonder these nations came to be known as the people of the buffalo!

Winters were hard on the plains.
The people set up camps close to rivers.
Some heaped earth around the bottom of
their tepees. Others built lodges of earth
to keep out the winter winds. Often there
was not much food.

Boys were sent out alone at night to fetch water.
Or they spent days and nights alone without food or water
to test their bravery. Boys of the plains nations wanted
to grow up to be good hunters and warriors.

They learned to make war whistles, war clubs, and
bows and arrows. They also learned to
shape bowls for pipes from stone and to
make stems from wood. A boy started work
as a moccasin-bearer or as a servant to a
warrior. Then he became a water-
carrier. After that he scouted for
herds of buffalo and kept
an eye out for enemies.
If he was a good scout he
became a warrior.

The best warrior
became the chief.

109

For play, the boys wrestled or rolled small hoops with spears. They spun tops and played stick ball. Their balls were made of deer or buffalo hair wrapped in strips of hide. Girls played house with toy tepees or carried puppies on their backs instead of baby dolls. And they helped their mothers.

East of the Mississippi River most of the land was covered with great forests. Many animals lived in the forests—bear and woodland buffalo and deer. The men of the woodland nations hunted these animals for food for their families.

PEOPLE OF THE
EASTERN
WOODLANDS

They also hunted smaller animals— rabbit, beaver, opossum, squirrel, and wild turkey. Boys of these nations learned to move silently through the forest so they could be good hunters. The men and boys also cleared trees and burned bushes.

In these clearings, the women and girls raised corn and beans and squash. They also gathered fruits and nuts and grass seeds and bulbs that were good to eat. In the fall, children gathered walnuts, hickory nuts, and acorns in the woods.

The woodland people liked to live together in villages. In summer many of them moved to summer homes near a lake or stream. They caught fish, turtles, and shellfish. When water birds flew south in the fall, the men caught some of them for food. Usually there was plenty to eat in the woods.

Homes were made of poles covered with bark or mud or grass mats to keep out the harsh weather. Some of them were round. They were called *wigwams* or *wickiups*. Other nations built long houses in which many families lived together.

Each family had its own cooking-fire and a space for a sleeping-shelf. In the cold winters people had more time to work indoors. They made fur robes and leggings and moccasins trimmed with porcupine quills. They made smoking pipes and tools, and decorations of shell beads.

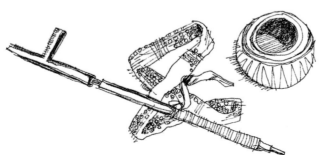

The women wove
baskets out of grass and
made boxes and pots
of birchbark. Canoes
were often made of birchbark, too.

While the families worked, the
old people told stories—about the
Great Spirit who watched over
them from the sky, about the Sun
which gave them life, about the Thunderbird
who roared from the clouds during storms and the
animals which gave them food—and

about the heroes of their people.

Some nations made mounds
of earth in the shape of snakes, eagles,
wildcats, and other animals for which
they had special respect. Grass grew
over these mounds and some can still be
seen today.

Paths led through the woodlands. Sometimes people of other nations came along those paths to trade furs, grain, or hard stone for arrow points. Many of the nations used strings of shell beads called *wampum* to pay for things they bought.

Nations spoke different languages. But they could speak together in sign language. Some Native Americans in the woodlands had fur and wild rice to trade. They did not raise crops. They were hunters and fishermen.

In the snowy winters they walked over the thick, soft snow on snowshoes. They pulled their wares on toboggans. Suits of furry hides kept them warm.

N orth of the woods, on the icy treeless plains, or *tundra*, other hunters and fishermen lived. They went to sea in skin boats to hunt whale, seal, and fish. On land they traveled in sleds pulled by husky dogs.

There were no trees to give them poles or bark for their homes. So they made houses of snow or chunks of earth rounded at the top over rafters of curved whale bone.

In the long dark winters they sat on their sleeping-shelves inside their warm sod or snow houses. They burned whaleblubber for light. Often they did not have much food.

The women and girls worked at softening hide for clothing by chewing it. The men and boys carved tools and decorations from stone, ivory, or bone. And the old people told stories.

South of the icy tundra, near the Pacific Ocean, deep forests grew. Nations in these forests fished and gathered shellfish from the sea. In the spring they went out in big canoes to hunt giant gray whales.

In the summer the woods gave them berries and fruit. This rich land could feed many families, so people lived in large villages. In the rainy, stormy winters they lived in the shelter of the forests. In spring and summer they paddled their canoes down the coast to summer homes.

They built sturdy wooden houses with posts carved from soft, tall cedar trees. Their canoes were made from cedar logs. And they carved tall poles into the shapes of the animals their families felt related to—deer, bear, turtle, beaver, or eagle.

Many village chiefs and others of these northwest coast nations became rich and powerful. They took pride in having gift-giving parties called *potlaches*. Many other nations also had ceremonies at which they gave gifts of blankets, shawls, baskets, and beadwork. The gifts honored those who got them. They also showed how rich the giver was. Sometimes in one great party a rich man of the northwest coast gave away all he owned! Of course he would soon be invited to someone else's potlach and be given fine gifts in return.

Parties, festivals, music, and dancing were very important to these people of long ago. At the center of almost any village was an open space for dancing. All year there were sun dances, rain dances, corn dances, deer dances, harvest dances, and winter dances.

Every nation had its own special dances. There were special dances to honor young people, both boys and girls, as they grew up.

Often dancers wore costumes. They wore masks to honor a spirit or god. And as a man danced, he seemed to become that spirit. To make music, people beat on painted drums, shook rattles made of dry gourds, and blew into whistles or pipes. Some of the best dances were those of the southwest nations who lived in bare, dry country where it was often very hot.

Some of the people of the southwest made simple shelters of thin posts or logs covered with brush or clay. But many nations built towns of high-piled houses made of stone or sun-dried brick.

PEOPLE OF THE
SOUTHWEST

Usually the town was built on top of a cliff or into the side of one, for protection. It was often a long climb to the town's small fields. There was little rain. Water for the corn, beans, and squash had to be brought from streams and pools by digging ditches.

Small boys and girls had long walks, too, taking the family flocks to pasture. These children of long ago had to learn to live with heat and cold, rain, snow, and hunger.

If sickness came, a medicine man was called. He brought herbs to cure the sickness or he called on good spirits to help. A sand painting could bring the spirits.

People of long ago lived close to the spirits of the earth and air and sea and sky. They believed that the land and waters belonged to everyone—to use and to enjoy—and to pass on to their children.

It was over five hundred years ago when sailing ships from Europe started to cross the ocean to this wide land. People of Europe saw the deep forests, the swift rivers, the grassy clearings. They liked what they saw and wanted it for themselves.

More and more of them came, bringing horses, wheels, guns, and many new ways of living. Since then life has never been the same for the nations of the first Americans.

FOLLOW THE DREAM
Peter Sis

O ver 500 years ago in the city of Genoa, in Italy, a little boy was born. His name was Christopher Columbus.

It was expected that Christopher would grow up to be a weaver, like his father.

But Christopher Columbus had his own ideas about his future.

He dreamed of the faraway places and people he read about in *The Travels of Marco Polo*.

He watched the ships in the harbor of Genoa and listened to the merchants and sailors as they unloaded their cargoes of exotic goods and spices brought from the Orient. And he kept weaving dreams of adventure and discovery.

As the years went by, Christopher Columbus formed a
plan. He would reach the Orient by a new route. Rather
than traveling east over a thousand miles of difficult terrain,
he would sail west, across the Atlantic Ocean.

Fulfilling his dream was not easy. He had to become an
expert sailor and had to learn how to read maps and the
stars for navigation.

He traveled throughout the Mediterranean and Europe,
looking for a sponsor to provide him with the ships, supplies,
and crew he would need for the long journey west.

Everyone thought Columbus's plan was too risky, or too expensive, or just impossible. But Columbus always expected that someday he would be granted his ships. He approached the King and Queen of Spain.

King Ferdinand and Queen Isabella listened quietly to Christopher Columbus, though his ideas about the world were so different from those of their advisers. They told him no.

Columbus had a second audience with the King and Queen, but it went no better than the first. His proposal to find a new trade route to the Orient by sailing west was rejected once more.

Six years later, Christopher Columbus was still the only one to believe that land lay to the west, across the ocean, and that riches would be found there.

But now Queen Isabella was intrigued. She offered the King her jewels as a token of her faith in Columbus's plan. Persuaded by his wife's conviction, the King decided to take a chance. He would provide Christopher Columbus with three ships and a crew of ninety men.

The ships were stocked with food and water and goods for trading.

Six months later, on August 3, 1492, the *Niña*, the *Pinta*, and the *Santa María* set sail from Palos, Spain.

The three ships headed west, taking advantage of the trade winds, which Columbus hoped would carry them directly to their destination. The sea was calm, and at first it seemed the journey would be easy.

But from the beginning the crew was uneasy. The endless expanse of sea, with its unfamiliar birds and fish and seaweed, frightened them. They wanted to turn back. Columbus was determined to keep sailing west.

In his cabin on the *Santa María*, Columbus kept the record of the voyage in the ship's log. But he actually kept two logs. In one, he shortened the distances to reassure the rebellious crew.

Day after day, through all kinds of weather, the three ships continued on their westward course.

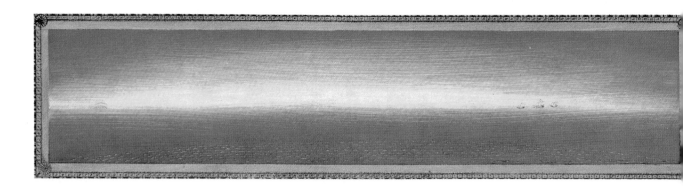

Then, on the seventy-first day, a little piece of land appeared on the horizon.

Columbus assumed it was part of Japan.

On October 12, 1492, just after midday, Christopher Columbus landed on a beach of white coral, claimed the land for the King and Queen of Spain, knelt and gave thanks to God, and expected to see the treasures of the Orient. . . .

Today we know that what Christopher Columbus found was not a new route to the Orient but a new continent. Columbus, however, never really knew that he had reached "America."

MEET PETER SIS, AUTHOR AND ILLUSTRATOR

Peter Sis says, "When I came to America in 1982, all I knew about Christopher Columbus was that he had sailed the ocean blue in 1492. Then I read many books about him and studied maps that he himself might have looked at. Some of them showed maps of Europe surrounded by high walls, with monsters standing guard beyond.

"Columbus didn't let the walls hold him back. For him, the outside world was not to be feared but explored. And so he followed his dream."

Sis was excited by Columbus's story because it reminded him of his own journey from Czechoslovakia to America.

SQUANTO AND THE FIRST THANKSGIVING

Joyce K. Kessel

illustrated by Lisa Donze

For thousands of years, people all over the world have set aside special days for giving thanks.

People in the U.S. and Canada have celebrated Thanksgiving for over 350 years.

How did Thanksgiving start? Most of us think right away of the Pilgrims, but the story really begins with a Native American, a Patuxet man named Squanto. Without Squanto, the Pilgrims would never have celebrated that first Thanksgiving.

The Patuxet people lived near the place we now call Plymouth, Massachusetts. There they grew corn and hunted wild animals. They were friendly and peaceful.

Then, in the early 1600s, an English ship came to Plymouth. These Englishmen were explorers. They were looking for riches. They hoped to find gold or silver, but all they found was corn and the Native Americans who lived there.

The Englishmen had never seen corn. They didn't know what to do with it. But they thought they knew what to do with the Native Americans. They would sell them as slaves!

So the Englishmen captured a few young Patuxet men. They took the Patuxets to England and sold them. Squanto was one of those Patuxets.

When he got to England, he was sold as a slave. He had to learn how to speak English, and he had to work very hard.

Squanto was used to hard work. The Plymouth winters were long and cold. Sometimes Squanto had been hungry all winter long. But the rest of the year had brought riches. The woods of his home were full of berries and wild animals. And even when he had been hungry, he had been free.

Squanto longed for his home. He dreamed of his people and of his wild, free land. His master could see that Squanto was not happy. He felt sorry for his slave. Finally he set Squanto free.

In 1614 Captain John Smith sailed for the place the Englishmen called the New World. Squanto went with him! He returned at last to his people. But not for long!

Captain Smith sailed back to England, but he left one of his ships behind. The captain of that ship was named Thomas Hunt. Hunt traded with the Patuxets. He filled his ship with fish and animal furs. But Hunt was greedy. He wanted to make more money than the fish and furs would bring. So he also filled part of his ship with Patuxet men. Squanto was captured again! After only a few weeks at home, he was sailing back across the ocean.

Hunt knew that Captain Smith would be angry with him for capturing the Patuxets. So Hunt sold the Patuxets in Spain instead of England.

Squanto's new masters were Catholic monks. They taught him the Christian faith. They were kind to him, but, of course, Squanto was sadder than ever.

All he wanted was his freedom. At last the monks took pity on him. They helped him get to England.

From England Squanto was able to find a ship going to America. He was on his way home again! But what great sadness he found when he arrived. Squanto could not believe his eyes! All the Patuxets were dead!

He wandered through empty villages. All he found were crumbling huts. The once-green cornfields lay black and dead. All the people were gone. Squanto was the only living Patuxet!

What had happened? People of a neighboring Native American nation told him. His people had all been killed by the "white man's plague." The ships from England had brought smallpox germs. Smallpox was a new disease to the Patuxets, so they died quickly from it. After all those years of longing for his home, Squanto found he had no home. He moved in with a neighboring nation.

S quanto had been back for one year when the Pilgrims landed at Plymouth, Massachusetts. That was on December 21, 1620. The Pilgrims were English. They had left England to look for a new home where people would let them worship God the way they chose. They were lucky to land at Plymouth. The Patuxets were all dead, and the other Native American people were afraid of smallpox. Because of this, there were not many Native Americans ready to fight for their land. The Native Americans just watched from a distance.

The Pilgrims had been townspeople. They did not know how to plant. They did not know how to build. They made cold, little houses out of mud, clay, and sticks.

They were not used to the cold, and they did not have much to eat. During their first terrible winter, half of the Pilgrims died. By the spring of 1621, there were only 55 of them left.

 130

That was when Squanto decided to help them. Squanto knew that the Pilgrims were Christians. None of the other Indians were Christians, but when Squanto had lived in Spain, he had become a Christian. Also, Squanto knew how to speak English. So in 1621 he went to visit the Pilgrims. After his first visit, he never left them.

Squanto taught the Pilgrims how to find animals to shoot for meat. He showed them how to build warm houses. He helped them make friends with the neighboring Native Americans. He explained how to plant. He told them to watch the leaves on the trees. When they were as big as squirrels' ears, the corn should be planted. He taught the Pilgrim women how to cook the corn.

131 ❦

Squanto and the Pilgrims worked very hard all spring and summer, and in the fall the harvest was a good one. Because of Squanto's help, the Pilgrims would have warm homes and plenty to eat through the winter.

The Pilgrims wanted to celebrate. They wanted to give thanks. They decided to have a feast. They sent Squanto to invite a Native American chief named Massasoit to their dinner. They thought that Massasoit might bring a few men too.

Thanksgiving feasts were not new to the Native Americans. Theirs was called the "Green Corn Dance," and it was a huge feast, so Massasoit brought 90 men to the Pilgrims' "Green Corn Dance!" The Pilgrims were very surprised, but they tried not to show it. There were 55 Pilgrims and 92 Native Americans. That made 147 people! The Pilgrims were not sure they had enough food for everyone. They had better get busy!

For three days the women did nothing but cook. When the day for the feast arrived, everything was ready.

What a feast it was! Massasoit and his people had brought five deer. The women made these into stew. They roasted turkeys, geese, and ducks. They cooked lobsters, eels, clams, oysters, and fish. They made biscuits and bread. They roasted corn for "hoe cakes."

They boiled corn with molasses to make "Indian pudding." There was plenty of dried fruit for everyone. There may even have been popcorn balls, since they were invented by the Native Americans in that area.

Usually the Pilgrims thought that games were a waste of time, but on this day they gave in. The men held contests. They leaped and jumped and raced.

Everyone showed off. The Pilgrim men marched, the Native Americans shot arrows, and, of course, people ate until they could hardly move.

What a joyous day that first Thanksgiving was. The Pilgrims had new, warm homes. They had new friends and plenty of food. They knew they would be able to live through the next winter. And none of it would have happened without a Patuxet named Squanto.

JAMES FORTEN, HERO AND TRUE FRIEND

Carol Siedell

illustrated by Eric von Schmidt

This is a true story. It happened in 1781.

James Forten and Daniel Brewton were friends living in Philadelphia. One day, they both decided to get jobs on the American warship *Royal Louis*.

They were hired as powder monkeys. Their job was to run in and out of the fodder room to get more gunpowder for the cannons. It was dangerous work, so anyone who worked as a powder monkey had to be brave.

Within months, their ship was captured by the British, and James and Daniel were taken prisoner.

On the British prison ship, Daniel became very ill. He was very afraid and he didn't think he would ever leave the boat alive.

But his friend, James Forten, did not worry. James had a plan for his own escape. He decided to hide in a sea chest that belonged to one of the enemy sailors. There would be barely enough room inside for one boy to fit into. James was sure that the sailor would be leaving the ship soon. The sailor would certainly carry his sea chest with him to shore. It would feel heavy, but the British would never know that there was a person inside. James could escape!

But then, James changed his mind and did something even more brave.

When James saw how ill his friend Daniel was, he decided to let him take his place. James slipped Daniel into the chest when no one was around.

When the sailor left the ship, the British let him take his chest along with him because they thought he had old clothes in it! James even helped lower the chest— with Daniel inside—down the side of the ship.

Daniel got well and was very happy to be free. But he worried about his friend James. He was afraid James would get in trouble and be sold as a slave. He remembered what James had told him once. He had said he would never be a slave. "I was born free," he always said.

James was set free three months later in New York. He walked all the way home to Philadelphia—115 miles.

When James Forten grew up, he became an expert at making sails for ships. He also became one of the richest men in Philadelphia. But he never gave up working to free slaves. He was born a free man and he believed everyone should be free also. Today, James Forten is remembered as a great businessman and a champion of freedom.

BUTTONS FOR GENERAL WASHINGTON

Peter and Connie Roop
illustrated by Peter E. Hanson

"Are any soldiers in the street, John?" his mother asked.

"Only the guard at General Howe's headquarters," John answered.

"Remember, John. Keep away from the British soldiers," his mother said. "And go the way I told thee."

"But I know a faster way," John said.

"Do as thy mother asks," his father said. "She has sent messages to General Washington before."

John nodded his head. He wished that his mother would finish sewing the new buttons on his coat. He was nervous and in a hurry to be on his way to General Washington's camp.

"Here, John," his mother said at last. "The new buttons look just like the old ones."

John took his coat. He ran his fingers over the cloth-covered buttons. He could not feel the small holes inside the buttons. Secret messages for General Washington were hidden in those holes.

"If I am caught, will anyone be able to read the messages?" John asked.

"No," answered his father. "I wrote them in a code that only thy brother Charles can read."

"I wish I could give the buttons to General Washington himself," John said.

"Maybe someday thee will," his mother said.

John carefully buttoned his coat.

"Be careful," his father warned. "The British are looking for American spies."

"If they catch thee, it means prison—or worse," his mother said.

A shiver ran down John's back. He knew that captured spies were lucky to end up in prison. Usually they were hanged. "I will be careful," John said.

"Here is thy pass to leave Philadelphia," his mother said. "Thou needs it to get past the British guards."

John put the pass in his pocket. His hands shook as he touched the buttons for good luck.

"We will wait supper for thee," his mother said.

"Godspeed, John," his father said.

John walked up Second Street. He turned on Market Street. British soldiers were everywhere. John wished they would all go back to England.

John walked slower as he neared the guardpost at the edge of town.

"Hey, Yankee Doodle," he heard a voice call from behind him. John turned quickly. It was Samuel Baker. Samuel's family liked the British soldiers. They wanted the British to win the war. The Bakers and other Tories wanted America to be part of England again.

John hated Samuel even more than he hated the British soldiers.

"Did you see all of our new soldiers?" Samuel asked. "You Americans can never win now. General Howe will whip Washington before Christmas."

"He will not," John said fiercely.

"Oh, yes, he will," Samuel said. "We British are too strong for you."

John stepped up to Samuel.

"Just thee wait and see who wins the war," John said angrily. "When we win, thee can return to England where thou belongs!"

"Who is going to make me?" Samuel said, poking John.

"Me!" John yelled.

Before John could move, Samuel hit him hard in the stomach. John fell down.

"See," Samuel said. "We will win." Samuel walked away proudly.

Brushing off his coat, John stood up. He wished he could hit Samuel back, even though he knew that he should not fight. Besides, he knew it was more important to reach General Washington's camp.

J ohn stopped at the guardpost. A red-coated British soldier took his pass. He looked at it for a long time. John began to worry.

"You are going to your aunt's house?" the soldier asked.

"Yes," answered John.

"I must check each pass carefully," the soldier said. "There are many American spies. You are not a spy are you?" the soldier asked with a smile.

"Oh, no, sir," John answered quickly.

"Off with you then," said the soldier. "Just remember, we hang any spies we catch."

Well, thou won't catch me, John thought as he put the pass back in his pocket.

John knew he should not be too sure of himself, though, so he kept a sharp lookout for more British soldiers. They might guess that he was a spy if they found him past his aunt's house. They might even find the secret messages.

John stopped suddenly. He heard horses coming. He
jumped over a ditch and hid behind a tree.

Five British soldiers came along the road. They passed
slowly. They were looking for someone.

John waited until the soldiers had ridden
away. He touched his buttons for good luck. A
button was missing!

John looked all over the ground. He could
not find the button anywhere. Then he
remembered Samuel Baker's blow. The button
must have come off near the guardhouse.

143

John started to run back down the road toward Philadelphia. His breath came in short gasps. He had to find that button.

He stopped near the guardpost. He looked all around for the button.

"Are you back so soon?" John jumped in surprise. The British guard walked toward him.

"I lost one of my buttons," John said. "My mother would not be happy if I could not find it."

The soldier held out his hand. He had John's button! "I found it where you boys were fighting," the soldier said.

John tried to keep his hands from shaking as he took the button. He hoped the soldier had not found the message. "Thank thee for finding my button," John said, backing away.

"On your way, then," said the soldier.

John put the button deep in his pocket. He looked at the sky. It was past noon.

Against his mother's warning, he took a shortcut through the woods toward General Washington's camp.

John stopped for a rest after an hour. He took a long drink from an icy stream. Suddenly, a hand grabbed him from behind as he stood up.

"What might you be doing in these woods?" asked a gruff voice.

John was spun around before he could answer. He faced a bearded man. The man aimed a pistol at John.

John said the first words that came to him. "I was hunting."

"Hunting without a gun?" the man asked.

"I was really going to my aunt's house," John said.

"I will take you with me to find out the truth," the man said sharply. "Now march," he ordered.

John knew that the man would shoot him if he tried to run. They walked through the woods for a long time. John was hungry and tired. He was scared, too. Where was the man taking him? What would John do if they were going to a British camp?

At last they came to an open field. A large white tent stood in one corner. Soldiers in blue uniforms were marching in the field. It was an American camp.

John breathed a sigh of relief. Once he talked to Charles, everything would be all right.

"We will have the truth from you now," the man told John. He took John to the white tent. "I have a spy here," the man told a soldier guarding the tent. "I caught him prowling in the woods near Philadelphia."

The soldier stepped into the tent. He was back within a moment. "Bring him in."

The bearded man pushed John into the tent.

"Sit down, son," said a tall man in a blue uniform. John sat in a wooden chair.

"They tell me you are a spy," the man said. "You are young for a spy. Whose side do you spy for?"

"General Washington's side," John said. "I am John Darragh. Charles Darragh is my brother. He helps General Washington. Can I see Charles now?"

The man turned to the soldier. "Send Charles Darragh to me at once."

John sat stiffly in front of the uniformed man. It seemed like a year

before Charles arrived. "Why, John," Charles said in surprise.

John smiled. Now he could prove that he spied for Washington. "Mother sent me. I have some messages for General Washington."

John took the loose button from his pocket. "There is a message in Father's code hidden inside."

Charles uncovered the button. He took out the message and looked at it.

"Please decode the message right away," the tall man said.

"Don't, Charles," said John. "Only General Washington is supposed to know."

Charles laughed at his brother. "John, this *is* General Washington."

General Washington held out his hand. John shook it. "It is an honor to shake the hand of so brave a patriot," the General said.

"Thank thee, sir," John said.

"Charles," said the General, "please report to me after you have decoded the messages." General Washington left the tent.

Charles began cutting the buttons off John's coat. John could not believe that he had met General Washington. Washington's words of praise still filled John's ears.

After removing the messages, Charles sewed the buttons back on John's coat.

"Now be careful on the way home," Charles said. "We need thee to bring more buttons."

John touched the buttons for good luck. Then he laughed as he put on his coat.

"I will bring enough buttons for General Washington's whole army!"

MEET PETER AND CONNIE ROOP, AUTHORS
Peter and Connie Roop hope to give children a peek into America's exciting past through their historical stories.

The Roops' love of travel helps to make their stories come alive. Walking along cobblestone streets in Philadelphia helped them to create the setting for Buttons for General Washington.

The Declaration of Independence. 1786. John Trumbull.
Oil on canvas. © Yale University Art Gallery

THE FIRST FOURTH OF JULY

from FOURTH OF JULY by Charles P. Graves
illustrated by Lydia Halverson

"Clang! Clang! Clang!" The music of the great bell floated over Philadelphia. It was calling the people to the State House yard. There they would hear a man read the Declaration of Independence.

Until 1776, the American colonies had been ruled by England. Now the Americans had decided to rule themselves. They would build a new nation.

It was a brave thing for the Americans to do. For they knew it meant a long war with England. England had a big army and navy.

When the people in Philadelphia heard the bell, they poured into the streets. They raced toward the State House. Most of them knew that Congress had voted for the Declaration on July 4. This was their first chance to hear someone read it.

As soon as the crowd gathered, the bell stopped ringing. A man stood up. He read the Declaration of Independence just as Thomas Jefferson had written it. Jefferson was a leader from Virginia.

The Declaration of Independence told the world why America wanted to be free. It told of the many unfair things England's King, George III, had done. And it said that the colonies were now independent.

"Hurrah!" the crowd shouted. Up in the State House tower a man rang the bell again. He thought of the words written on it.

"Proclaim liberty throughout all the land, unto all the inhabitants thereof."

These wonderful words are from the Bible. The bell they are written on is now called the Liberty Bell. The State House is now Independence Hall.

News of the Declaration of Independence spread slowly throughout America. It went by men on horseback and by boat. There were no telephones or radios then.

153

General George Washington was in New York City. A copy of the Declaration was sent to him. He had it read to his soldiers.

The American soldiers had already been fighting the English. They had been fighting for their rights. Now they had something greater to fight for—freedom!

The soldiers knew this meant a hard fight. They felt sure they could win. We call the war they fought the Revolutionary War.

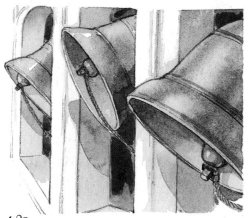

There was a big statue of King George III in New York. It was made of lead. Some of the American soldiers pulled the statue down. They cut off the statue's head. The lead from King George's statue was made into bullets. The Americans fired the bullets at the King's soldiers.

In many other towns people pulled down royal statues. Sometimes they tied ropes around the necks of the statues. Then they pulled the statues through the streets.

When news of the Declaration reached Boston, the people went wild with joy. American soldiers fired their cannon in honor of the thirteen American states. "Boom! Boom! Boom!" roared the cannon, thirteen times in all.

Bells rang. Drums beat. The people pulled down all signs that said George III was their king. They made a big bonfire out of the signs. They danced around it happily.

News of America's independence spread to all the states. Finally a copy of the Declaration reached a little settlement in South Carolina. Not many people there could read.

But a nine-year-old boy, Andrew Jackson, had learned to read in school. The grownups met at a farmhouse to hear him read the Declaration.

The grownups clapped when they heard the boy say *"all men are created equal."* They cheered when he read that everyone has a right to *"Life, Liberty and the pursuit of Happiness."*

The United States was born on July 4, 1776. America's birthday is her biggest holiday.

FINE ART
OUR COUNTRY:
THE EARLY YEARS

The Puritan. 1899. Augustus Saint-Gaudens.

Bronze. Membership Purchase Fund, Herbert F. Johnson Museum of Art,
Cornell University. 72.83

 156

The Spirit of '76. c. 1880.
A.M. Willard.

Oil on canvas. Collection
of the Board of Selectmen, Abbot Hall,
Marblehead, Massachusetts

Beaded shoulder bag. c. 1750.
Chippewa (Great Lakes).

National Museum of the American Indian,
Smithsonian Institution, Washington, D.C. 2321

The Oregon Trail. 1869. Albert Bierstadt.

Oil on canvas. The Butler Institute of American Art, Youngstown, Ohio

THE PIONEERS
Marie and Douglas Gorsline

I n the early 1800s, many people wanted to settle the land west of the Mississippi River. The most adventurous of these were called pioneers.

Some pioneers who went to the Far West—Oregon, Santa Fe, and California—were used to moving west little by little, searching for better farmland. Others came from the East or from Europe. If they had enough money to spare, they could load their wagons onto flat-bottomed steamboats and ride in comfort up the Missouri River to the frontier. Beyond the frontier lay a vast unsettled territory.

The pioneers of the Oregon Trail usually began their journey at the frontier town of Independence, Missouri.

They started coming in early spring, when the weather was best for traveling. They camped in their wagons outside of the town, where families joined together to form wagon trains. By traveling in groups, they could help and protect each other on their journey across unknown lands.

For most of the year Independence was a quiet town. But during the months of April and May it was filled with excited farmers and their families getting ready to head west. They listened to stories of the men who had made the trip before—traders, trappers, soldiers, mountain men, and missionaries.

The trip by car to Oregon today takes five or six days. There are places to stop on the highway—gas stations, motels, restaurants, and stores. But the pioneers' trip would take five or six *months!* And there were very few places to stop. In Independence they could buy the food, tools, and clothing they would need along the way. They also bought what they needed to start a new life in the West.

Most pioneers on the Oregon Trail drove an ordinary farm wagon. Their supplies were protected from the sun, wind, and rain by a canvas top. It was stretched over hickory branches lashed to the wagon's sides. Though the large wooden wagon wheels were clumsy and made turning difficult, they allowed the wagons to pass over big rocks and go through shallow water without getting wet. Pioneers going to California, and most of the traders on the trail, rode in Conestoga wagons, which were twice as long as a farmer's wagon.

The pioneers' wagons carried food, tools for the trip and tools for farming, clothing, cooking pots, medicine, guns, and whatever household goods and furniture the pioneers could make room for. They made extra space inside by sewing pockets in the canvas to hold small things. But after a wagon was loaded, there was little room left for passengers. And the ride was so bumpy that almost everyone preferred to walk.

Fifty to seventy-five wagons and more than three hundred people—a wagon train was a mile-long village on wheels, with all the problems of village life to face. Before starting out, the people elected leaders to run the train. They also hired guides, who knew the trail well, to map the best route west. The daily work was divided up.

Some men scouted the land for good campsites, some hunted game for food, and others tended the animals.

Three or four teams of strong, sturdy oxen were needed to pull each of the pioneers' wagons, which were called *prairie schooners*. As they set out across the prairie, the wagons looked like a fleet of schooner ships sailing on the ocean.

The pioneers risked their lives against all kinds of dangers. But they had the faith and courage to try to make their dreams of a better life come true.

They traveled twelve or fifteen miles a day. Women and children walked alongside the wagons, gathering stones, flowers, and berries. Life was different from "back home." There were still many chores to do, and the children had to help. But there was no school! The only classroom was the great outdoors, with its vast, ever-changing landscape to explore.

At noon and at night the wagon train stopped as close as possible to wood and water. The wagons formed a circle to protect the people in case of an attack and to keep the animals from straying. The oxen were unhitched to graze and drink. Hunters brought back game to be cooked. Everyone ate sitting on the ground around the campfires.

As the pioneers neared the treeless plains, wood became more scarce. The children had to gather dry buffalo dung, "buffalo chips," for the cooking fires. Pits were dug for the fires and the pots were hung over them.

After dinner, the pioneers amused themselves with talking and games, music—if there was a fiddler along—and knitting and quilting. While the people slept in tents or in their wagons, a night watch guarded the camp until dawn.

Storms were the greatest danger to the pioneers on the open prairies. Wagons were easy targets for lightning. A heavy rain could swell the streams, which flooded the land and turned the earth to mud. Then the wagons

might be stuck for hours, or days! High winds could easily blow over a wagon. And a storm could frighten the pioneers' livestock, causing the animals to run off in alarm.

As the weeks passed, the pioneers moved west under a hot summer sun. There was less drinking water and less grazing land for the animals. Hot, dry weather caused the wagon wheels to shrink and crack. The iron rims loosened and fell off. If the train was lucky enough to have a blacksmith along, he made repairs quickly so the wagons could roll once more.

Life on the prairie was very tiring and usually just plain dull. Seeing a stagecoach was a cause for great excitement. During the short time the Pony Express carried the mail to and from California, spotting one of its riders was a high point of the trip.

163 ❧

After crossing many rivers and streams, the pioneers came to the South Platte River. Like other rivers of the plains, it was shallow but dangerous to cross. The river might be flooded by storms. It had hidden deep spots and quicksand traps. The oxen didn't like the water and they often refused to cross. If the oxen stopped moving midstream, a man could drown trying to turn the stubborn beasts around. The rushing water could carry the oxen downstream—and the wagons with them!

As the westward trail climbed higher, it passed through the strange rock formations of the Badlands. Soon the wagons came to their first stop, Fort Laramie. In the early years of the wagon trains, the Native Americans nearby were friendly. They camped around the fort and traded buffalo robes for goods they could get at the well-stocked fort.

Inside the fort the pioneers could buy supplies they had run out of, refresh themselves and their animals, and have their wagons repaired. For the first time in weeks, they could do their laundry! Though they had been over a lot of rough trail—almost seven hundred miles—they had gone only one-third of the way. The hardest parts were yet to come!

In the later years of the wagon trains, the Native Americans saw the pioneers taking their lands and killing off the buffalo. Native Americans of the Plains depended on the buffalo for their food and clothing. They became angry and began to attack more frequently. The pioneers usually tried to protect themselves by locking their wagons in a circle. But attacks almost always came as a surprise, and many pioneers and Native Americans lost their lives in battle.

After leaving Fort Laramie, the pioneers crossed wild volcanic deserts with huge rock formations. Then, suddenly, they reached a broad, green valley—the South Pass. This was the first place north of New Mexico where they could cross the Rocky Mountains. Though they had traveled long and far, they were still more than halfway from their goal.

The pioneers had to be out of the mountains before the heavy snows trapped them there. The oxen were getting tired and worn out. To make the going easier, the pioneers threw some of their belongings out of the wagons. As the trip wore on, many people became sick and died. Some of the pioneers turned back. But most of them kept up their hopes. Young people fell in love and married. Babies were born on the trail.

Pioneers going to Oregon had miles and miles of steep slopes and gullies and huge rocks to travel around. Many wagons broke beyond repair, forcing families to double up. Sometimes they could use spare parts from one wagon to fix another. But the oxen pulling the wagons suffered from strains or falls, and many of them died.

Worst of all the mountain hazards was getting caught in a blizzard. The snow fell heavily in the high mountain passes, stranding wagons and their families. Stuck in snowdrifts, with no place to seek cover, the pioneers could freeze to death or meet up with hungry wild animals looking for food.

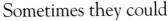

When the pioneers reached the Columbia River, they faced more hardships and a difficult choice—to travel by land or water. River travelers had to build a boat or raft and hope it would be sturdy enough to get their wagons and possessions through the dangerous rapids. They had to leave their animals behind.

167

Those pioneers who wanted to keep their herds to raise in Oregon stayed on the land. They hoped it would be safer. But they had mile-high, snow-capped mountains in their path, and many of them lost nearly everything. Of the 340,000 pioneers who traveled the Oregon Trail, nearly 20,000 lost their lives.

The pioneers who made their way through the last great mountain range before the Willamette River Valley had a wonderful view of the land they had struggled so hard to reach.

Between them and the coastal mountains lay a beautiful valley with lots of timber, rich soil, and plenty of water. The climate was mild, and the river was good for transportation. Fish and game were plentiful.

Most important, there was more than enough good land to farm and to build on. But the pioneers still had a lot of back-breaking work to do.

The pioneers arrived in Oregon in October, during the rainy season. Often working in rain and mud without proper tools, they had to move rocks, fell trees, and chop logs for houses and fences. And they continued to live in their wagons. But they looked forward to the spring, when they could begin to plant their crops. Soon the Oregon Territory was covered with fields and dairy farms and towns. The pioneers had finally made their dream of a better life come true.

BIBLIOGRAPHY

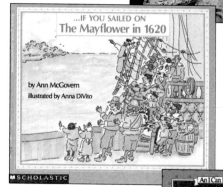

 170

Indians: The First Americans by Kathryn F. Ernst. Who are the Native Americans who have lived in our country from long, long ago? Find out about the first Americans in this interesting book.

Christopher Columbus: A Great Explorer by Carol Greene. Read about Christopher Columbus, who was not the first to discover America—people already lived there—but who was a great explorer. This is his exciting story.

. . . If You Sailed on the Mayflower *in 1620* by Ann McGovern. Who were the Pilgrims? Where does their story begin? What kind of ship was the *Mayflower?* Find the answer to these questions and more in this exciting book about the *Mayflower.*

George the Drummer Boy by Nathaniel Benchley. Read about a young British drummer boy who finds himself in the first skirmishes of the Revolutionary War.

The Boston Coffee Party by Doreen Rappaport. Follow the two courageous sisters who helped Boston women stand up to a greedy merchant during the Revolutionary War period.

Yankee Doodle by Dr. Richard Schackburg. Find out how the Revolutionary War era song "Yankee Doodle" came to be written, and sing along with some of the verses.

The Star-Spangled Banner by Peter Spier. Do you know who wrote our national anthem and what inspired him? You can find out in this exciting story how our national anthem came to be.

We the People by Peter Spier. Pictures of colonial and modern life make this book about the meaning of the U.S. Constitution even more interesting.

OUR COUNTRY: E PLURIBUS UNUM

173

OUT OF MANY PEOPLE, ONE NATION

Wiley

174

The United States of America has a long history. It is more than two hundred years old. But many other countries were already hundreds of years old when the United States was born. So you could say that the United States is still a very young country. It is made up of many different groups of people, who have come from all over the world. In the next few pages, you will hear about some of these people.

Many people think that Columbus was the first European to discover America. He was Italian, but his voyage was paid for by Spain. When he arrived in 1492, a lot of people were already living here. They had been at home here for thousands of years.

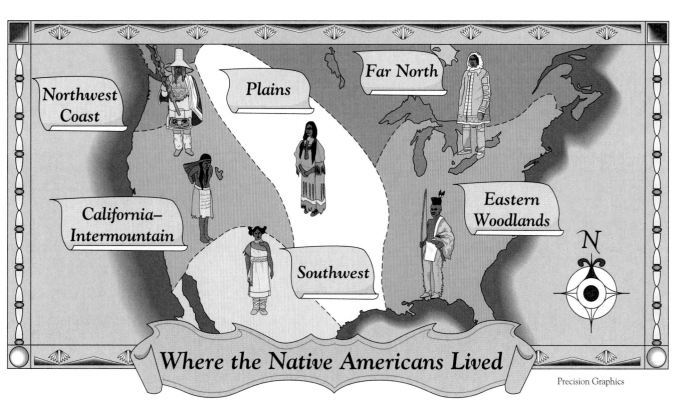

Northwest Coast

Plains

Far North

California–Intermountain

Eastern Woodlands

Southwest

N

Where the Native Americans Lived

Precision Graphics

The people lived in many different groups and nations, all over North and South America. We now call them Native Americans because they were already living in America when Columbus arrived. But Columbus thought he had arrived in East Asia, which people in Europe called the "Indies." So he called the people he found here "Indians."

For a hundred years after Columbus arrived, Spain and Portugal were the only countries that sent people to explore America. Most of the explorers went to South America, where they found gold. They also found silver in the place that we now call Mexico.

175

Spain wanted to own the gold and silver. Explorers and soldiers were sent from Spain to claim the gold and silver. They made the native people into slaves. Many died. Their great cities and temples were destroyed. But Spain became rich and powerful. The king of Spain became the most powerful king in the world. He ruled over many lands around the globe.

About seventy-five years after Columbus arrived in America, Spain built the first European settlement, or colony, in the land that is now called the United States. The first Spanish town was called St. Augustine. It is still a town today. More Spanish people arrived in the same area, and Spain called its colony *Florida*. Today that colony is the state of Florida.

The Bettmann Archive

After another fifty years or so, English settlers began to arrive farther north. The first two English colonies were Jamestown, founded in 1607, and Plymouth, founded in 1620. Plymouth was founded and settled by the Pilgrims. Their ideas about worship had not been accepted in England. The English government did not like their way of life. The Pilgrims' lives were threatened, and sometimes the Pilgrims were beaten up. So they went to Plymouth, where they could worship as they pleased.

Some Native Americans welcomed the early settlers, and helped them. They taught the settlers about the land and how to farm. But not all Native Americans were happy to give up their land. Often the newcomers were unfriendly, too. They brought guns and violence, and new diseases that killed many Native Americans.

Settlers from all over Europe came to the new colonies. They came from France, Germany, Sweden, Ireland, and Scotland. Each of these groups went to different places. Many of the Germans settled in Pennsylvania. Delaware was first settled by people from Sweden.

Precision Graphics

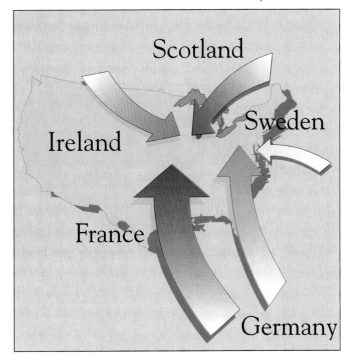

These people came to America for many reasons. Some came for freedom to do as they pleased, like the Pilgrims. Others came because they were poor. They had no land in their old country, and wanted some land to call their own. Others came as indentured servants. An indentured servant had to work for seven years for a single master. In return, he was given food and housing. At the end of the seven years, the servant was free.

Many indentured servants were brought from Africa. Some came of their own free will, but most were forced. The great plantations of the southern colonies needed more workers than could be found in America.

Plantation owners began to buy slaves from Africa. Slaves were tied up and crowded into the lower decks of ships, like animals. Many were treated very badly by the plantation owners. While indentured servants became free in time, slaves had no hope of freedom. But they survived, and kept their African roots.

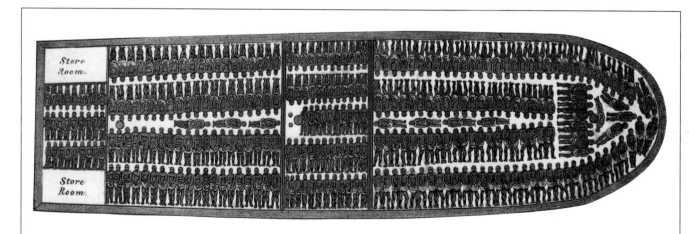

The Bettmann Archive

Gershom Griffith

The King of England wanted to be more powerful. He needed more money. He tried to get money from his American colonies by making the colonists pay him many taxes. It didn't work. The colonies resisted. They refused to pay. In fact, they declared themselves a separate country, independent of England. On 4 July 1776, the English colonies became the United States of America. The King sent over an army to stop this. But the new country fought back. France helped out, too. The King of England lost the war, and his colonies remained the separate country called the United States.

More and more people came to the new country, mostly from Europe. Many were poor and wanted land of their own. The first thirteen colonies were getting crowded. More and more of the newcomers went west to find land. By 1850, many went as far west as the Pacific Ocean. They went to a place the Spanish had settled long before, called California.

179

It was very hard to get to California from the East. Some went by wagon train. Others went by ship. Both ways were dangerous, and took a long time. Then, in the 1860s, a railroad was built to connect California with the eastern states. It was a lot of work. There weren't enough people to do all that work. Workers were brought in from all over the world to help. Many came from China and stayed in the United States after the railroad was finished.

Many different groups have made this country their home. Most of us are newcomers. Our families have only been here for a hundred years or so, or sometimes even less than that. Sometimes our families came to seek opportunities. Sometimes they were forced to come here. But all of us live together in the same country now.

People keep coming to live in the United States because of the land and jobs they can find here. They come from all over the world. People from Poland, Russia, Greece, Mexico, Korea, Vietnam, India, and Africa have made the United States their home. Others are still coming from many different places. All groups bring with them new ideas and talents.

This makes the United States different from most countries. Most countries have only one or a few groups of people. In those countries, many families have stayed in the same place for a thousand years, or more. The

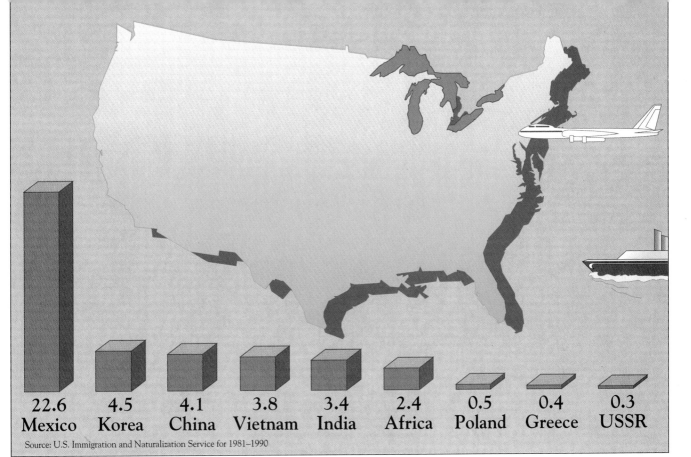

| 22.6 | 4.5 | 4.1 | 3.8 | 3.4 | 2.4 | 0.5 | 0.4 | 0.3 |
| Mexico | Korea | China | Vietnam | India | Africa | Poland | Greece | USSR |

Source: U.S. Immigration and Naturalization Service for 1981–1990

In this picture, you will see the names of places with boxes above them. Most newcomers to the United States come from one of these places. The boxes tell us how many newcomers out of each hundred come from each place.

Precision Graphics

181

United States is different. Our families are mostly newcomers. We came from many different places.

The motto of the United States is *e pluribus unum*. (You can find it on any of our coins.) That means "out of many, one." Out of many groups of people, we have made one nation. Each group has helped to make the United States what it is today.

ABRAHAM LINCOLN

David A. Adler

illustrated by John and Alexandra Wallner

Abraham Lincoln was born on February 12, 1809, in a one-room log cabin in Kentucky. Abraham and his older sister Sarah helped in the house and on the farm. When they were not needed at home, they walked two miles to school and two miles back.

When Abraham was seven years old his family moved farther west, to Indiana. Abraham helped his father chop down trees. They cleared the land for their farm and built a new log cabin.

When Abraham was nine his mother died. A year later his father married Sarah Bush Johnston, a widow with three children. Abraham's new stepmother was good to Abraham. He called her "my angel mother."

Abraham loved books. Sometimes he walked many miles to borrow one. When he plowed the fields he often stopped to read.

In 1830, when Abraham was twenty-one, his family moved to Illinois. Abraham helped his father plant corn and build a fence and a new house.

Abraham was tall and thin. He was also very strong. In 1831, he and two other men built a flatboat. They floated it down the Mississippi River to New Orleans.

In New Orleans Abraham saw a slave market for the first time. Black slaves in chains were being sold like cattle. Seeing that done to people made Abraham miserable. He never forgot what he saw.

Abraham took a steamboat up the river to New Salem, Illinois, where he worked as a clerk in a general store. He was twenty-two years old. Abraham laughed, told jokes and stories, and loved to talk about politics. People liked him.

In 1834, Abraham Lincoln began to study law. Two years later he became a lawyer and moved to Springfield, the new capital of Illinois.

Abraham ran for public office many times. He served in the Illinois legislature. For two years he was also a member of the United States House of Representatives.

In Springfield Abraham fell in love with Mary Todd. She was lively and smart. They were married in 1842.

They had four sons, Robert, Edward, William and Thomas.

In 1858, Abraham was chosen by the new Republican party to run for the United States Senate. He ran against Senator Stephen A. Douglas.

Abraham Lincoln spoke out against slavery. He and Senator Douglas had many debates. Lincoln lost the election, but the debates made him famous throughout the country.

In 1860, Abraham Lincoln ran against Senator Stephen A. Douglas for president of the United States. This time Abraham Lincoln was elected.

When Abraham Lincoln became president there were more than three million black slaves in the southern states. Voters in the South were not happy to have a president who hated slavery.

Soon after Abraham Lincoln was elected president eleven southern states withdrew from the United States. They formed their own government, the Confederate States of America.

On April 12, 1861, Confederate soldiers fired on Fort Sumter, a United States fort in South Carolina. The war between the North and South, the Civil War, began.

Abraham Lincoln led the war to keep the country united.

During the war Lincoln wrote the Emancipation Proclamation. It declared that all slaves in the Confederate states were free.

In 1863, Lincoln spoke at Gettysburg, Pennsylvania. His speech became known as the Gettysburg Address. He said our government "of the people, by the people, for the people, shall not perish from the earth."

In 1864, the North won some important battles. Later that year Abraham Lincoln was re-elected president.

On April 9, 1865, the war ended. The South surrendered to the North. The war had lasted four years. Many had died.

Five days later, on the evening of April 14, Abraham and Mary Lincoln were at the theater. One hour after the play began there was a shot. John Wilkes Booth, an actor who favored the South, had shot the president. Lincoln died the next day.

A train carried Abraham Lincoln's body to Springfield, Illinois. Millions of Americans came to watch the train pass by, to say good-bye to Abraham Lincoln.

People called him "Honest Abe," "Father Abraham" and "Savior of the Union." Some say Abraham Lincoln was our greatest president.

The Bettmann Archive

189 ❧

MEET DAVID A. ADLER, AUTHOR

David Adler didn't start out to be a writer. He was always good in math and taught it for nine years before becoming a full-time author. Adler says, "I made up stories to entertain my younger brothers and sisters. I'm still making up stories." Adler has many interests, such as math, science, history, riddles, mysteries, adventure stories, and biographies. He writes about these interests in his books.

INDIAN CHILDREN LONG AGO
Nancy Byrd Turner

Where we play in field and hill,
Running high and low,
Other children used to play,
Long and long ago.

Little Indians straight and slim,
Boys with belt and feather,
Little girls with colored beads,
Playing all together.

Laughing, calling through our yard
(When 'twas field of maize),
Swift and light they used to run,
Back in other days;

Through our garden (once a wood)
In and out again,
Past the house they ran, and back—
'Twas a wigwam then.

Sometimes when the air is clear,
On a quiet day,
We can almost hear them still,
Shouting at their play!

BUFFALO DUSK
Carl Sandburg

The buffaloes are gone.
And those who saw the buffaloes are gone.
Those who saw the buffaloes by thousands and how they
      pawed the prairie sod into dust with their great hoofs,
      their great heads down pawing on in a great pageant
      of dusk,
Those who saw the buffaloes are gone.
And the buffaloes are gone.

illustrated by Stella Ormai

LA FLORIDA
Thekla von Schrader
illustrated by Gail Piazza

For centuries, the only people living on the land we now call Florida were Native Americans. About 10,000 Native Americans lived there during the early 1500s.

After Columbus landed in a small group of islands between North and South America, explorers from many countries in Europe traveled through what is now North America. Most of these explorers went home sooner or later. A few stayed in North America and built little towns where they could live together. These little towns in the new land, where groups of people coming from the same country lived, were called colonies, or settlements.

Some of the people came from the countries of England and Holland to live in what is now Massachusetts. They were called Pilgrims.

But the Pilgrims were not the first Europeans to build permanent settlements in this land. Many years before the Pilgrims landed at Plymouth Rock, Spanish people had built a colony called St. Augustine. It was the very first permanent European colony in the United States.

The first European to explore Florida was a Spaniard named Juan Ponce de León. He was born in Spain, but he came to America at the age of nineteen. He sailed to America in 1493, on a voyage with Christopher Columbus. For several years, he lived in a Spanish settlement in the West Indies.

In 1508, Ponce de León decided to explore a nearby island. After he and his crew of explorers discovered gold there they decided to stay. They became the first Spanish people to live there, in what is now called Puerto Rico. The Spaniards went to war with the Arawak Indians who were then living on the island. When the Spaniards won the war in 1509, Ponce de León became the island's first governor.

Ponce de León became rich and powerful, but in 1512 his enemies fired him from the job of governor of Puerto Rico. Ponce de León had enjoyed being a rich and powerful man. He tried to think of ways to keep his riches.

For a long time, many stories were told in both Europe and America about a magical Fountain of Youth. Ponce de León remembered stories that the fountain was on the island of Bimini. He heard tales of old people who bathed in the fountain and became young again. The stories even said that the fountain could make sick people well.

It was only a story, of course. The Fountain of Youth was not a real fountain. Ponce de León did not know this, though. He believed that the stories might be true, and he wanted very much to find the fountain. He knew that if he found it, it would bring him a great deal of money.

People who were old or sick would pay him large amounts of money for a chance to bathe in the Fountain of Youth.

The King and Queen of Spain also believed the story of the Fountain of Youth. They gave Ponce de León money to look for Bimini and make it part of the Spanish empire.

In 1513, Ponce de León took a group of explorers to the area we now call Florida. Much of this area is surrounded by water. Ponce de León thought that Florida was an island. He hoped that it was the island of Bimini.

Ponce de León and his crew landed very near the place that later would become the colony of St. Augustine. It is located in northeastern Florida. Ponce de León sailed from St. Augustine all the way down the eastern coast of Florida, looking for the fountain.

195

He explored Florida's eastern shoreline on the way. He did not find the Fountain of Youth there, so he got back in his boat and sailed partway up the western coast of Florida.

Ponce de León never did find the Fountain of Youth. In spite of this, he wanted the land he had explored to become part of the Spanish empire. He named the land *La Florida*. The word *florida* means "full of flowers" in Spanish. One story says that Ponce de León chose this name because of the many flowers he saw in Florida. Another story says that Ponce de León chose the name *Florida* because he landed in Florida at Easter time. In Spain the Easter season is called *Pascua Florida*.

Ponce de León and his followers did not stay long in Florida. Angry Native Americans, afraid of losing their land, drove the Spanish out.

Many years later, a group of French people settled near what is now Jacksonville, Florida. The King of Spain sent an army to drive the French out. When the French left, many of the Spanish people decided to stay. They called their colony St. Augustine. It became the first permanent European settlement in what is now the United States.

In time, Florida became part of the United States. Today, the first colony is a city. It is still called St. Augustine.

EAST MEETS WEST

Jennifer Johnson
illustrated by Pamela Johnson

In the mid-1800s, there were no airplanes or cars. The fastest and easiest way to travel was by train. Most people living in the United States during that time lived in the East. They could travel by railroad from one eastern city to another. The trips took a few days or less. The rides were usually safe and comfortable.

198

Not many people lived in the American West at this time. There were almost no large cities in the West, but the region was growing quickly.

In 1848, gold was discovered in a river in California. Many people traveled to California to mine for gold, hoping to become rich.

Other people moved west so that they could have land of their own. The East was getting crowded, and land there was expensive. In the West, there was plenty of land, and the land was cheap and sometimes even free.

Traveling from East to West was not as easy as going from one eastern city to another. No railroad tracks linked the settled East with the West, so people could not go west in a train. They had to travel on horseback or by covered wagon. A trip to the West took many months and was hard and dangerous. Along the way many people got sick and died. Many others were killed by bandits, by wild animals, or in fights with Native Americans.

Then, in the 1860s, the United States government hired two companies to build a railroad that would connect the East with the West. The Union Pacific Railroad would lay tracks going west from the last station at Omaha, Nebraska. The Central Pacific Railroad would lay tracks going east from Sacramento, California. When these two sets of tracks met, the railroad would be finished. The rails were to link up and form one line, tying in with the railroads that were already in use in the eastern part of the country.

Building railroads was rough, dangerous work. The Central Pacific company had trouble finding enough men to do the work. Most men who went to California were there only to find gold. But many Chinese men in California badly needed jobs and money.

Most of the Chinese in California came from a place in China near the city of Canton. The soil there was very thin and rocky. The farmers could not grow enough crops to feed all the people who lived in the area.

Soon after gold was discovered in California, the Chinese in Canton heard about it from American sailors. Thousands of young, poor Chinese men sailed to America, hoping to become rich in the "gold mountains" of California. They could then send their riches to their

starving families in China. Most of these men, however, hoped to move back to China someday.

Not everyone in California was happy to see the Chinese. Dressed in baggy cotton clothing and large straw hats, the Chinese did not look like other Californians. Chinese men wore their hair in a long braid. Also, when they first arrived in America most of them could not speak English.

Some people were afraid the Chinese would take too many of the good jobs. So, the Chinese could get only the lowest-paying jobs. They were hired to clean houses and cook meals. When the railroad project began, many Chinese men wanted to work on the railroad to make decent wages.

Two years after the Central Pacific project started, the man in charge of the company badly needed workers. Many of his men had quit to do easier or higher-paying jobs. Only a few miles of track had been laid. He did not want to hire Chinese workers as replacements. But finally he decided to try a small crew of fifty Chinese workers. The crew worked so hard and so well that the Central Pacific company decided to hire many more Chinese men. Within a few months, the company had hired 3,000 Chinese workers and was looking for even more.

The Central Pacific did not treat its Chinese workers the same way it treated its other workers. White workers were paid thirty-five dollars a month. The Chinese began working for only twenty-six dollars a month. The Chinese had to work for a couple of years before they earned the same pay as everyone else. The Central Pacific gave meals to all its crews—except the Chinese. They had to get their own meals. The Chinese also worked longer days

than the other crews. The Central Pacific expected
Chinese crews to work from sunrise until sunset. They
worked at least twelve hours every day.

In 1865, Chinese crews began clearing a path through
the High Sierras. That winter there were forty-four
snowstorms in the mountains. The Chinese worked in
snow as high as their waists. They slept in cotton tents
that gave them little protection from the weather.

Often, avalanches—sudden falls of large amounts of snow and rocks—roared down the mountainsides.

The biggest problem the Chinese faced in the mountains, though, was the dangerous job they had to do. They had to cut tunnels through the mountains where the railroad tracks would be laid.

When the crews worked on the steep mountainsides it was often impossible to find a foothold. Sometimes they had to gather on a flat cliff top, and then lower workers down the mountainside in baskets tied to long ropes.

The workers in the baskets drilled holes in the mountainside and filled the holes with gunpowder. When they set the gunpowder on fire, the explosion cleared away a large chunk of the mountain at once.

This method was very dangerous for the workers in the baskets. As soon as the gunpowder was lit, other workers pulled the baskets back up the mountain. But sometimes the other men did not pull fast enough, and the explosions killed the Chinese workers in the baskets. Other times the ropes broke and the basket riders fell down the mountainside.

When the dangerous job in the mountains was finally complete, the workers moved on to the Nevada desert. Here it was blazing hot in the summer. When the winter came again, the temperature sometimes dropped as low as 50 degrees below zero.

The Chinese workers had had enough. In 1867, 2,000 of them went on strike, asking for shorter hours and more pay. The Central Pacific said, "Work—or starve!" The company cut off the Chinese crews' supplies of food and water. The Chinese had no choice. They were forced to go back to work.

On 10 May 1869, the Central Pacific work crews met the crews from the Union Pacific Railroad at Promontory Point, Utah. The first railroad to cross the continent of North America was completed! The East and West were linked.

A famous photograph shows workers from the two railroad companies together at Promontory Point. Although four out of five Central Pacific workers were Chinese, there are no Chinese men in the photo. Even though the Chinese did so much of the work on the railroad, no one noticed them or thanked them for their work.

Many of the Central Pacific's Chinese workers stayed in America for the rest of their lives, and others from their country joined them here. Some Chinese men continued to do railroad work even though it was hard and dangerous. Others became farm workers or fishermen. Some opened restaurants or laundries.

Today, Chinese Americans live in many different parts of the country. They have continued to contribute to the growth of our nation, not only through the railroads, but also in many other ways, such as in the fields of agriculture, medical science, and engineering.

Bruce Lee
Actor

Connie Chung
Anchorwoman

Lawrence Yep
Writer

Michael Chang
Tennis player

FINE ART
OUR COUNTRY:
E PLURIBUS UNUM

Eagle. 1980. Stan Hill.

Mohawk, Six Nations Reserve, Ontario, Canada.
Moose antler. Iroquois Indian Museum,
Howes Cave, New York

Our Banner in the Sky. 1861.
Frederic Edwin Church.

Oil on paper mounted on cardboard. Daniel J. Terra
Collection, Terra Foundation for the Arts. 1922.27.
Photo: ©Terra Museum of American Art, Chicago.

 208

Black Cowboys. 1972–1974. Kwasi Seitu Asantey.

Acrylic on canvas. Membership Purchase Fund,
Herbert F. Johnson Museum of Art, Cornell University. 74.83

WATCH THE STARS COME OUT

Riki Levinson
illustrated by Diane Goode

Grandma told me when her Mama was a little girl she had red hair—just like me.

Grandma's Mama loved to go to bed early and watch the stars come out—just like me.

Every Friday night, after the dishes were put away, Grandma's Mama would come to her room and tell her a special story.

When I was a little girl, my big Brother and I went on a big boat to America. Mama and Papa and Sister were waiting there for us.

My aunt, Mama's sister, took us to the boat. She didn't bring my two little brothers. They were too small. They would come on a boat when they were older.

Aunt gave us a barrel full of dried fruit. She asked an old lady to watch over us. And she did. She also ate our dried fruit.

The old lady and Brother and I went down the steps to our room. I counted the steps as we carried our bundles down, but there were so many, I forgot to count after a while.

Sometimes the boat rocked back and forth—it was fun! Some people didn't like it—they got sick. The old lady got very, very sick. She died.

Brother told me not to worry. He would take care of me—he was ten.

At night when I went to sleep, I couldn't see the stars come out in the sky. That made me sad.

Each morning when we got up, Brother put a mark on his stick. I counted them—twenty-three.

The last morning we looked across the water. There were two islands near each other. One of them had a statue standing on it—a lady with a crown. Everyone got very excited and waved to her. I did too.

When the boat stopped, we carried our bundles down the plank.

I started to cry. I did not see Mama and Papa and Sister. A sailor told me not to worry—we would see them soon.

We went on another boat to a place on an island.

We carried our bundles into a big, big room. Brother and I went into a small room with all the other children without mamas and papas.

A lady looked at me all over. I wondered why.

I waited for Brother. The lady looked at him too.

The next day we went on a ferry. The land came closer and closer as we watched. Everyone waved. We did too.

Mama and Papa and Sister were there!

We went on a trolley to our home. Mama said it was
a palace.

Mama's palace was on the top floor. I counted the
steps as we walked up—fifty-two!

Mama and Papa's room was in the middle. Our room was in the front. And in the back was the kitchen with a big black stove.

Mama warmed a big pot of water on the stove. She poured some into the sink and helped me climb in to wash.

Mama washed my hair, and when it was dry, she brushed it. It felt good.

Sister gave us cookies and glasses of tea.

I was very tired.

I kissed Mama and Sister good-night. Papa patted me
on my head and said I was his little princess.

I went into our room and climbed into Sister's bed.
It was right next to the window.

I watched the stars come out. One, two, three.

This Friday night I will go to bed very early and watch the stars come out in the sky.

I hope Grandma will come to my room and tell me another special story.

219

MEET RIKI LEVINSON, AUTHOR

Riki Levinson says, "Until September of 1983, I had never written a story since high school. One day I told my husband that I had an idea for a story but that I didn't know how to write. And he said, 'Don't worry about writing— just put it down.' My very first story was Watch the Stars Come Out.*"*

MARTIN LUTHER KING, JR.

David A. Adler

illustrated by Robert Casilla

Martin Luther King, Jr., was one of America's great leaders. He was a powerful speaker, and he spoke out against laws which kept black people out of many schools and jobs. He led protests and marches demanding fair laws for all people.

Martin Luther King, Jr., was born on January 15, 1929, in Atlanta, Georgia. Martin's father was a pastor. His mother had been a teacher. Martin had an older sister, Willie Christine, and a younger brother, Alfred Daniel.

Young Martin liked to play baseball, football, and basketball. He liked to ride his bicycle and to sing. He often sang in his father's church.

Young Martin played in his backyard with his friends. One day he was told that two of his friends would no longer play with him, because they were white and he was black.

Martin cried. He didn't understand why the color of his skin should matter to anyone.

221

Martin's mother told him that many years ago black people were brought in chains to America and sold as slaves. She told him that long before Martin was born the slaves had been set free. However, there were still some people who did not treat black people fairly.

In Atlanta, where Martin lived, and elsewhere in the United States, there were "White Only" signs. Black people were not allowed in some parks, pools, hotels, restaurants, and even schools. Blacks were kept out of many jobs.

Martin learned to read at home before he was old enough to start school. All through his childhood, he read books about black leaders.

Frederick Douglass

Harriet Tubman

George Washington Carver

Martin was a good student. He finished high school two years early and was just fifteen when he entered Morehouse College in Atlanta. At college Martin decided to become a minister.

After Martin was graduated from Morehouse, he studied for a doctorate at Boston University. While he was there he met Coretta Scott. She was studying music. They fell in love and married.

In 1954 Martin Luther King, Jr., began his first job as a pastor in Montgomery, Alabama. The next year Rosa Parks, a black woman, was arrested in Montgomery for sitting in the "White Only" section of a bus.

Dr. Martin Luther King, Jr., led a protest. Blacks throughout the city refused to ride the buses. Dr. King said, "There comes a time when people get tired of being kicked about."

One night, while Dr. King was at a meeting, someone threw a bomb into his house.

Martin's followers were angry. They wanted to fight. Martin told them to go home peacefully. "We must love our white brothers," he said. "We must meet hate with love."

The bus protest lasted almost a year. When it ended there were no more "White Only" sections on buses.

Dr. King decided to move back to Atlanta in 1960. There, he continued to lead peaceful protests against "White Only" waiting rooms, lunch counters, and rest rooms. He led many marches for freedom.

In 1963 Dr. King led the biggest march of all—the March on Washington. More than two hundred thousand black and white people followed him. "I have a dream," he said in his speech. "I have a dream that my four children will one day live in a nation where they will not be judged by the color of their skin but by the content of their character."

The next year in 1964, Dr. King was awarded one of the greatest honors any man can win, the Nobel Peace Prize.

The country was changing. New laws were passed.
Blacks could go to the same schools as whites.
They could go to the same stores, restaurants, and
hotels. "White Only" signs were against the law.

Dr. King told his followers to protest peacefully. But
there were some riots and some violence.

Then, in April 1968, Dr. King went to Memphis, Tennessee. He planned to march so black and white garbage workers would get the same pay for the same work.

On April 4 in Memphis, Dr. King stood outside his motel room. Another man, James Earl Ray, was hiding nearby. He pointed a rifle at Dr. King. He fired the gun. An hour later Dr. King was dead.

227

Martin Luther King, Jr., dreamed of a world free of hate, prejudice and violence. Carved on the stone which marks his grave are the words, "I'm free at last."

BIBLIOGRAPHY

Abraham Lincoln by Kathie Billingslea Smith. Find out what Abraham Lincoln was like when he was growing up and how he became one of our most famous presidents.

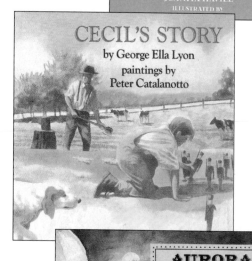

Treasure Nap by Juanita Havill. On an afternoon when it is too hot to sleep, a young girl asks to hear the story about how her great-great-grandmother came to the United States from Mexico, bringing a special treasure.

Cecil's Story by George Ella Lyon. A boy imagines what it would be like if his father went off to fight in the Civil War. What would happen to him? How would his life change?

Aurora Means Dawn by Scott Russell Sanders. Travel with a family in a covered wagon to find a new home. Live their adventures and the excitement of settling in a brand-new region.

My Prairie Year by Brett Harvey. What was it like for settlers living on the prairie when our country was young? Read about it in this book based on the journals of Elenore Plaisted, an actual pioneer woman.

The Quilt Story by Tony Johnston and Tomie de Paola. Follow the story of a beautiful quilt that a pioneer mother stitches to warm her daughter Abigail. Many years later another mother mends the old quilt for her little girl.

The Long Way Westward by Joan Sandin. What would it be like to go live in a new and strange country? Read about two young brothers and their family who arrive in New York from Sweden and travel to their new home in Minnesota.

Lion Dancer: Ernie Wan's Chinese New Year by Kate Waters and Madeline Slovenz-Low. Ernie Wan lives in Chinatown in New York City. In this book, Ernie invites us into his home to show and tell how he celebrates the Chinese New Year.

GLOSSARY

230

account (ə kount´) *n*. A reason.

adviser or **advisor** (ad vī´ zər) *n*. A person whose job is to give opinions and information to someone important, such as a king or queen.

agriculture (ag´ ri kul´ chər) *n*. Farming.

anxious (angk´ shəs) *adj*. Very eager; wanting to do something.

arm (ärm) *v*. To get weapons for fighting.

assume (ə so͞om´) *v*. To say or think that something is true without knowing; to suppose.

bearer (bâr´ ər) *n*. A person who carries something.

biography (bī og´ rə fē) *n*. The story of a person's life.

boycott (boi´ kot) *v*. To refuse to buy someone's products; to refuse to do business with someone.

brass (bras) *n*. A shiny, gold-colored metal.

brush (brush) *n*. A thick bunch of leaves, bushes, and other plants in a forest.

brush

camomile (kam´ ə mīl´) *n.* A kind of tea that is like a medicine.

campsite (kamp´ sīt´) *n.* A place to live outdoors or in tents.

canopy (kan´ ə pē) *n.* A light, overhead covering supported on poles.

canvas (kan´ vəs) *n.* A strong, rough cloth used to make tents.

century (sen´ chə rē) *n.* One hundred years.

character (kar´ ik tər) *n.* A person's honesty and honor.

charcoal (chär´ kōl´) *n.* Wood that has been burned until it is black.

city-state (sit´ ē stāt´) *n.* A city that is also a country. A city-state includes land and villages just outside the city.

clog (klog) *n.* A wooden shoe.

coastal (kōs´ tl) *adj.* Having to do with the land next to the sea.

code (kōd) *n.* Words or signs that have a secret meaning.

congratulations (kən grach´ ə lā´ shənz) *interj.* Said when one is happy for someone's success.

Congress (kong´ gris) *n.* The group of people who are elected to make laws in the United States; the House of Representatives and the Senate together.

continent (kon´ tn ənt) *n.* One of the seven large bodies of land on the earth.

contribute (kən trib´ yōot) *v.* To give something; to help.

conviction (kən vik´ shən) *n.* A strong belief; something that a person believes firmly.

crew (krōo) *n.* A group of people who work together.

currant (kûr´ ənt) *n.* A berry that grows on a bush and can be eaten.

dairy farm (dâr´ ē färm´) *n.* A place where cows are kept to produce milk.

231

debate (di bāt´) *n.* An argument or discussion in which the two sides give formal speeches.

decode (dē kōd´) *v.* To change a secret message into its real meaning.

defend (di fend´) *v.* To protect; to keep safe; to keep attackers from winning.

demand (di mand´) *v.* To say that something should belong to one; to claim as one's own.

depend (di pend´) v. To trust; to expect that someone will do something.

destination (des´ tə nā´ shən) n. The end of a journey; the goal.

doctorate (dok´ tər it) n. An award for graduating from the highest level of college; a doctoral degree.

downstream (doun´ strēm´) adv. In the same direction that the water flows in a river.

drive (drīv) v. To force to move.

dusk (dusk) n. Twilight; nightfall; the time when the sky is just getting dark.

dye (dī) v. To color.

ebony (eb´ ə nē) n. A dark, heavy wood.

elect (i lekt´) v. To choose by voting.

election (i lek´ shən) n. The process of choosing someone by voting.

emerald (em´ ər əld) n. A green gem; a jewel that is green.

empire (em´ pīr) n. A group of countries that are under the same ruler.

engineering (en´ jə nēr´ ing) n. The science of designing and building machines, bridges, and roads.

exert (ig zûrt´) v. To use one's strength.

exotic (ig zot´ ik) adj. Strange or unusual.

expanse (ik spans´) n. A wide, open space.

expect (ik spekt´) v. To demand; to order.

explore (ik splor´) v. To look all over an area of land for the first time.

fable (fā´ bəl) n. A story that teaches a lesson; a legend.

favor (fā´ vər) v. To be kind to.

fell (fel) v. To knock down; to cut down.

ferry (fer´ ē) n. A boat that carries people and things across a river or a bay.

fiction (fik´ shən) n. A story that is made up or imagined.

fit (fit) adj. Good enough; suitable; right.

fleet (flēt) n. A group of ships.

flint (flint) *n.* A very hard stone that can be used to start fire.

fodder (fod´ ər) *n.* The raw material that goes into making a product.

foothold (foot´ hōld´) *n.* A place to put one's feet.

forlorn (for lorn´) *adj.* Without friends; alone.

fortnight (fort´ nīt´) *n.* Two weeks; fourteen nights and days.

found (found) *v.* To start.

fountain (foun´ tn) *n.* A source of water; a spring.

fountain

frame (frām) *n.* A glass-covered structure placed over young plants in a garden to protect them from the cold.

frontier (frun tēr´) *n.* The place where the wilderness begins.

game (gām) *n.* Wild animals hunted for food.

general store (jen´ ər əl stor´) *n.* A store in a country area that sells many different kinds of things.

globe (glōb) *n.* The planet Earth.

gourd (gord) *n.* A family of hard-shelled fruits such as melons.

graze (grāz) *v.* To eat grass.

guardhouse (gärd´ hous´) *n.* A building for soldiers who are on duty protecting an area; a guardpost.

gully (gul´ ē) *n.* A deep channel in the ground worn by a stream.

hardship (härd´ ship) *n.* Trouble; misfortune.

hazard (haz´ ərd) *n.* A danger.

headquarters (hed´ kwor´ tərz) *n.* The place where the leader of soldiers gives commands.

herb (ûrb) *n.* Any flowering plant used in cooking or as a medicine.

hide (hīd) *n.* The skin of an animal.

homeland (hōm´ land´) *n.* The country in which a person was born.

horizon (hə rī´ zən) *n.* The faraway line where earth and sky seem to meet.

233

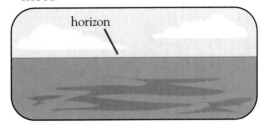
horizon

Pronunciation Key: at; lāte; câre; fäther; set; mē; it; kīte; ox; rōse; ô in bought; coin; boŏk; tōo; form; out; up; tûrn; ə sound in about, chicken, pencil, cannon, circus; chair; hw in which; ring; shop; thin; thˍere; zh in treasure.

House of Representatives (hous´ uv rep ri zen´ tə tivs) *n.* A part of Congress; one of two groups of people who are elected to pass laws for the United States. The other group is the Senate.

hull (hul) *n.* The body of a ship.

imitate (im´ i tāt´) *v.* To copy.

implore (im plor´) *v.* To beg.

inhabitant (in hab´ i tənt) *n.* One who lives in a place.

inscription (in skrip´ shən) *n.* Something written on stone or another hard surface.

intrigued (in trēgd´) *adj.* Deeply interested.

knave (nāv) *n.* A person who is not honest; a villain.

lacquer (lak´ ər) *n.* A hard, shiny coating.

lane (lān) *n.* A narrow road.

lash (lash) *v.* To fasten; to tie tightly.

lawyer (lô´ yər) *n.* A person who has studied laws and helps people go to court.

lead (led) *n.* A heavy, dull-colored metal.

legislature (lej´ is lā´ chər) *n.* A group with the power to make laws.

liberty (lib´ ər tē) *n.* Freedom.

livestock (līv´ stok´) *n.* Farm animals.

lodge (loj) *n.* One type of Native-American home.

loom (lōōm) *n.* A machine for weaving cloth.

magnificent (mag nif´ ə sənt) *adj.* Grand; superb; splendid.

maize (māz) *n.* Corn.

midstream (mid´ strēm´) *n.* The middle of a river.

mine (mīn) *v.* To dig in the earth.

minister (min´ ə stər) *n.* 1. A person who helps a king or queen rule. 2. A pastor; the leader in a church.

mischief (mis´ chif) *n.* Trouble that a child gets into.

missionary (mish´ ə ner´ ē) *n.* A person whose job is to get other people to follow his or her religion.

moccasin (mok´ ə sin) *n.* A soft shoe made of deerskin, first made and worn by Native Americans.

molasses (mə las´ iz) *n.* A thick syrup.

monk (mungk) *n.* A man who lives a religious life in a place that is away from the everyday world.

motto (mot´ ō) *n.* Words that tell something important about a group such as a country or state.

navigation (nav ´ i gā´ shən) *n.* The act of steering a ship.

newcomer (nōō´ kum´ ər) *n.* Someone who has recently arrived.

nonfiction (non fik´ shən) *n.* Literature or stories that are true.

opal (ō´ pəl) *n.* A precious stone that seems to change color when it is turned in the light.

opossum (ə pos´ əm) *n.* A small, furry animal that lives in trees and pretends to be dead when it is in danger.

opportunity (op´ ər tōō´ ni tē) *n.* A good chance; a favorable time.

oxen (ok´ sən) *n.* The plural of **ox:** A large, strong animal in the cattle family, used to pull heavy loads.

oxen

pageant (paj´ ənt) *n.* A colorful parade or display.

pass (pas) *n.* A way to go over a mountain.

patriot (pā´ trē ət) *n.* A person who is loyal to his or her country.

perish (per´ ish) *v.* To die.

permanent (pûr´ mə nənt) *adj.* Lasting; enduring; staying.

persuade (pər swād´) *v.* To convince; to cause to agree with one.

plague (plāg) *n.* A disease that many people catch in a short time.

plank (plangk) *n.* A wide, thick, flat piece of wood used for walking across.

plantation (plan tā´ shən) *n.* A very large farm where one large crop is grown. The workers usually live on the property.

Pronunciation Key: at; lāte; câre; fäther; set; mē; it; kīte; ox; rōse; ô in bought; coin; bŏŏk; tōō; form; out; up; tûrn; ə sound in about, chicken, pencil, cannon, circus; chair; hw in which; ring; shop; thin; there; zh in treasure.

politics (pol´ i tiks) *n.* All the things people do to get elected to government or to work in government.

postbox (pōst´ boks´) *n.* A mailbox; a container for mail.

prairie (prâr´ ē) *n.* A large area of land covered with grass.

prejudice (prej´ ə dis) *n.* Unfairness; an opinion formed without knowing the facts.

procession (prə sesh´ ən) *n.* A group of people marching in line; a parade.

proclaim (prō klām´) *v.* To say to the public; to declare.

proposal (prə pō´ zəl) *n.* A plan offered by someone.

protest (prō´ test) *n.* An objection; a complaint.

public office (pub´ lik ô´ fis) *n.* A job to which a person is elected.

pursuit (pər sōōt´) *n.* The act of trying to get something.

236

puzzled (puz´ əld) *adj.* Confused.

raft (raft) *n.* A lot of something.

rafter (raf´ tər) *n.* A long piece of wood or some other strong material used to hold up a roof.

rapids (rap´ idz) *n.* A swift-running part of a river.

rapids

re-elect (rē´ i lekt´) *v.* To vote into office again.

rebellious (ri bel´ yəs) *adj.* Refusing to obey.

reflected (ri flek´ tid) *adj.* Bounced back from another place.

reject (ri jekt´) *v.* To refuse.

relief (ri lēf´) *n.* The feeling when a person gets rid of a worry or a problem.

Republican party (ri pub´ li kən pär´ tē) *n.* A political group in the United States.

resist (ri zist´) *v.* To oppose; to hold out against something.

respect (ri spekt´) *n.* Honor; admiration; approval.

retold (rē tôld´) *v.* Past tense of
  retell: To tell again; to repeat; to
  say again.

rewrite (rē rīt´) *v.* To write again in a
  different way.

right (rīt) *n.* Something that
  everyone is allowed; something that
  is due to a person.

rim (rim) *n.* The outer circle of a
  wheel.

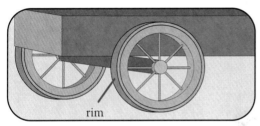

rogue (rōg) *n.* A rascal; a scoundrel; a
  cheater.

roots (rōōts) *n.* The first home and
  family that a person had; a person's
  family history.

route (rōōt) *n.* The way traveled; the
  path to something.

ruby (rōō´ bē) *n.* A red gem; a jewel
  that is red.

sand-bank (sand´ bangk´) *n.* A large
  amount of sand.

sapphire (saf´ īr) *n.* A blue gem; a
  jewel that is blue.

savior (sāv´ yər) *n.* One who rescues
  or saves.

scarce (skârs) *adj.* Hard to get; rare.

schooner (skōō´ nər) *n.* A sailing
  ship.

scout (skout) *n.* A person whose job
  is to go out and find out what is
  going on away from home. —*v.* To
  gather information.

Senate (sen´ it) *n.* A part of
  Congress; one of two groups of
  people who are elected to pass laws
  to run the United States. The other
  group is the House of
  Representatives.

settle (set´ l) *v.* To move into.

sieve (siv) *n.* A container with a
  bottom made of many crossed wires,
  used for separating small pieces from
  larger ones.

237

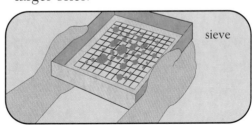

slight (slīt) *adj.* Small; not important.

sod (sod) *n.* A piece of earth with
  grass growing in it, pulled away from
  the ground.

Pronunciation Key: at; lāte; câre; fäther; set; mē; it; kīte; ox; rōse; ô in bought; coin; bŏŏk; tōō; form; out; up; tûrn; ə sound in about, chicken, pencil, cannon, circus; **ch**air; **hw** in **wh**ich; ri**ng**; **sh**op; **th**in; **th**ere; **zh** in treasure.

spectacles (spek′ tə kəlz) *n.* Eyeglasses; glasses to help one see better.

sponsor (spon′ sər) *n.* A person who pays the costs for an event or project.

stagecoach (stāj′ kōch′) *n.* A vehicle people ride in that is pulled by horses.

steamboat (stēm′ bōt′) *n.* A boat driven by a steam engine.

strain (strān) *v.* To overdo; to work a muscle so hard that it is hurt.

strand (strand) *v.* To leave helpless.

strike (strīk) *n.* A stopping of work.

surrender (sə ren′ dər) *v.* To give up.

survive (sər vīv′) *v.* To keep living in spite of hardships or difficulties.

suspect (sə spekt′) *v.* To not trust; to think that something is wrong.

talent (tal′ ənt) *n.* A natural skill or ability.

tax (taks) *n.* Money that people pay to their government to run the country.

temple (tem′ pəl) *n.* A place where people pray.

terrain (tə rān′) *n.* An area of land with all its natural features.

territory (ter′ i tor′ ē) *n.* A large area of land.

thee (thē) *pron.* You.

thong (thông) *n.* A strip of leather that goes between the toes to hold on a shoe or sandal.

thou (thou) *pron.* You.

thy (thī) *pron.* Your.

timber (tim′ bər) *n.* Trees to be used for wood; lumber.

toboggan (tə bog′ ən) *n.* A long, narrow sled for coasting downhill over snow or ice.

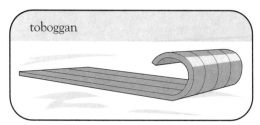

toboggan

Tory (tor′ ē) *n.* A person who was on the side of the British during the American Revolution.

train (trān) *n.* A long end of a robe that drags on the ground.

238

trolley (trol´ ē) *n.* A bus that runs on rails powered by electricity, often called a streetcar.

'twas (twuz) Contraction of *it was.*

unexpectedly (un´ ik spek´ tid lē) *adv.* By surprise.

unfit (un fit´) *adj.* Not good enough to do a job; not suitable; not right.

united (yo͞o nī´ tid) *adj.* Joined together.

unwary (un wâr´ ē) *adj.* Not careful; not cautious.

upset (up set´) *v.* To knock over.

vast (vast) *adj.* Huge; enormous.

volcanic (vol kan´ ik) *adj.* Created by the earth throwing out smoke, ashes, and melted rock.

ware (wâr) *n. usually* **wares:** Goods; things that are made.

warship (wor´ ship´) *n.* A very large ship with weapons for fighting.

wheelbarrow (hwēl´ bar´ ō) *n.* A light, one-wheeled cart for moving heavy loads.

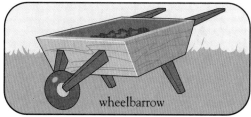
wheelbarrow

whip (hwip) *v.* To beat eggs.

widow (wid´ ō) *n.* A woman whose husband has died.

withdraw (with drô´) *v.* To go away from.

wove or **woven** (wōv) or (wō´ vən) *v.* A past tense of **weave:** To make something by putting long, thin strips over and under each other. Thread is used to make cloth; straw or grass is used to make baskets.

239

COLOPHON

*This book has been designed in the classic
style to emphasize our commitment to classic
literature. The typeface, Goudy Old Style, was
drawn in 1915 by Frederic W. Goudy, who based it
on fifteenth-century Italian letterforms.*

*The art has been drawn to reflect the golden age
of children's book illustration and its recent rebirth
in the work of innovative artists of today.
This book was designed by John Grandits.
Composition, electronic page makeup, and photo
and art management were provided by
The Chestnut House Group, Inc.*